Paul Carter

English
with... **games**
and **activities**

ELi

© 2002 - ELI s.r.l.
P.O. Box 6 - Recanati - Italy
Tel. +39/071/75 07 01 - Fax +39/071/97 78 51
www.elionline.com
e-mail: info@elionline.com

Illustrated by Roberto Battestini
English version by Paul Carter and Karen Mackie

Adapted from *L'Italiano con giochi e attività*
by Federica Colombo

All rights reserved.
No part of this publication may be reproduced in any form or by any means or for any purpose without the prior permission of ELI.

Printed in Italy - Tecnostampa Recanati - 02.83.227.0

ISBN 978-88-8148-821-6

Introduction

English with games and activities is designed for elementary students of varying ages, studying English as a foreign language.

There are 3 volumes in the series and each volume contains games and activities which help students to gradually acquire basic vocabulary and grammar.

There are **14 units** in each volume and each unit deals with a different vocabulary topic. There are about 20 illustrated words on the first page of each unit. These words are then used on the following five pages in various **games and activities** such as crosswords, word searches, anagrams etc.

At the end of each unit a grammar point is introduced, followed by various related exercises using vocabulary from the unit.

The appendix contains **Solutions** to all the exercises so that students can use the books without supervision.

In the house

roof

chimney

garden

garage

door

window

hall

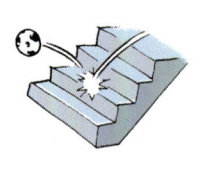

stairs

kitchen

living room

bathroom

bedroom

study

wall

cellar

1 Look at the picture and write the words.

2 Look at the pictures and put the letters in the correct order.

1. Philip sleeps in the ....
   M O B D E O R

2. He watches television in the ....
   V L I R M O I O G N

3. He eats in the ....
   N T H C I K E

4. He washes his face in the ....
   A B H R M O T O

5. He uses the computer in the ....
   Y S U T D

In the house

5

3 Do the crossword.

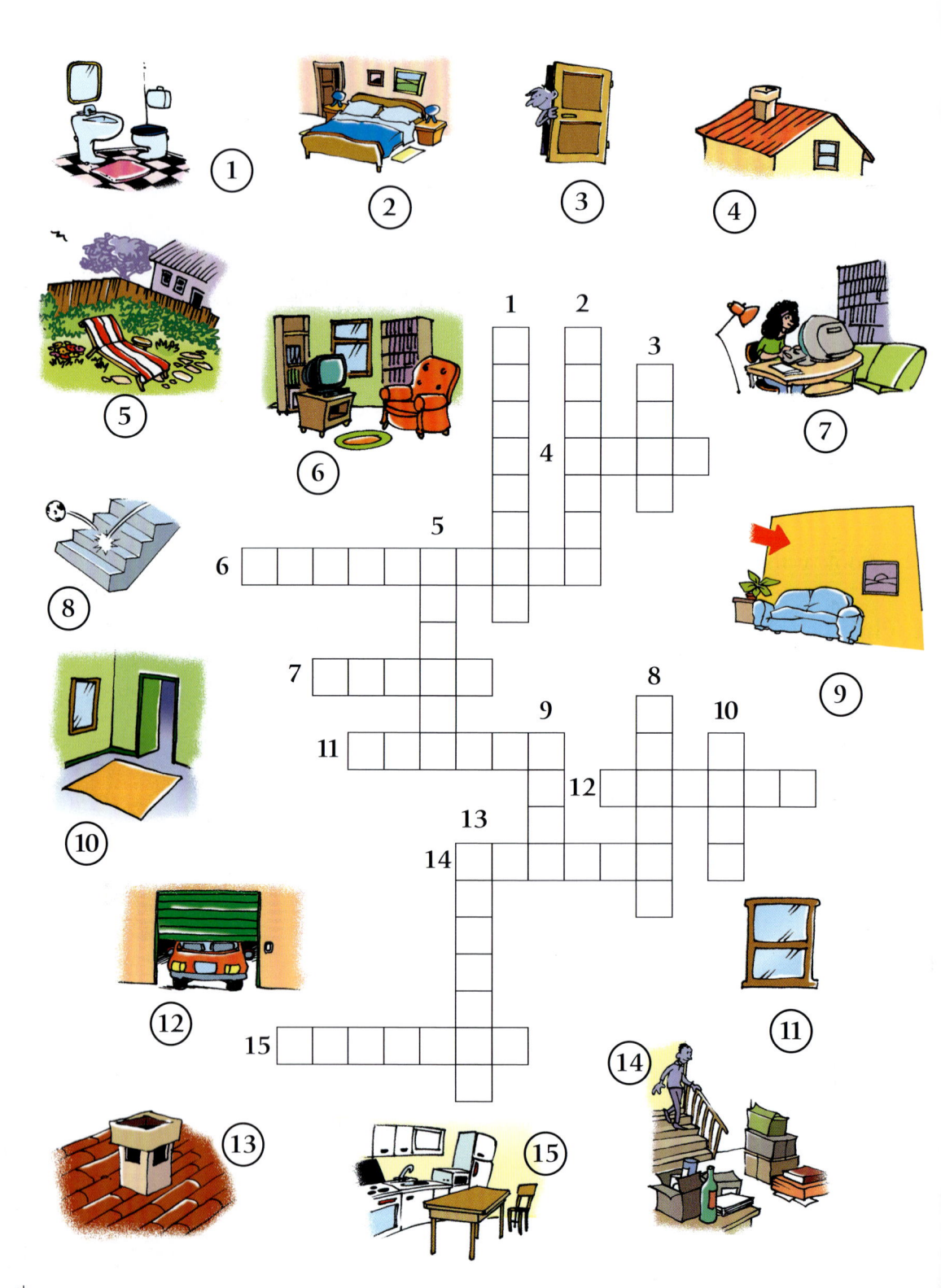

4 Look at the pictures and complete the sentences.

1.  "Can you open the .... please?"

2.  John is having a birthday party in the ....

3.  "I'm going downstairs to get a box from the ...."

4.  Mr Brown is coming out of the .... in his car.

5.  A tree damaged the ....

6.  Mr Graham is hanging a picture on the ....

7.  The bedroom .... is open.

8.  Smoke is coming out of the ....

9.  Nick is running up the ....

10.  Tom is sleeping in the ....

5 What rooms are there in this flat? Write the numbers beside the words.

◯ kitchen
◯ bedroom
◯ bathroom
◯ living room
◯ hall
◯ study

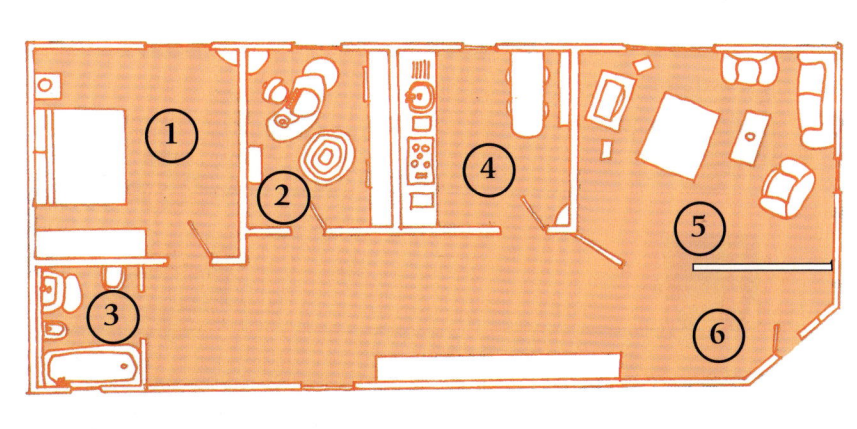

In the house

6 Look at these houses and write sentences.

A

What is there in house A?
There is a kitchen.
There are two bathrooms.
There is a ....
....

There are ....

B

What is there in house B?
There is a ....
....
....
....
....

There are ....

7 Look at the pictures and write 6 sentences with *there is/there are*.

There is one kitchen in my house.

1. .... 4. ....

2. .... 5. ....

3. .... 6. ....

A skyscraper always has a lot of floors…

30th	thirtieth
29th	twenty-ninth
28th	twenty-eighth
27th	twenty-seventh
26th	twenty-sixth
25th	twenty-fifth
24th	twenty-fourth
23rd	twenty-third
22nd	twenty-second
21st	twenty-first
20th	twentieth
19th	nineteenth
18th	eighteenth
17th	seventeenth
16th	sixteenth
15th	fifteenth
14th	fourteenth
13th	thirteenth
12th	twelfth
11th	eleventh
10th	tenth
9th	ninth
8th	eighth
7th	seventh
6th	sixth
5th	fifth
4th	fourth
3rd	third
2nd	second
1st	first

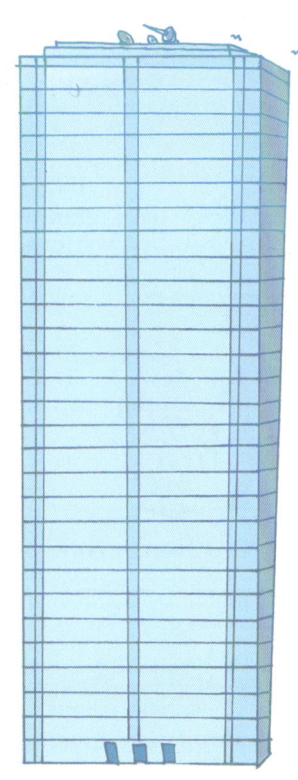

Describe your house.

8 If you live in a flat, what floor do you live on?

....

9 Write the corresponding ordinal numbers in the grid, then complete the sentence with the letters in the grey squares.

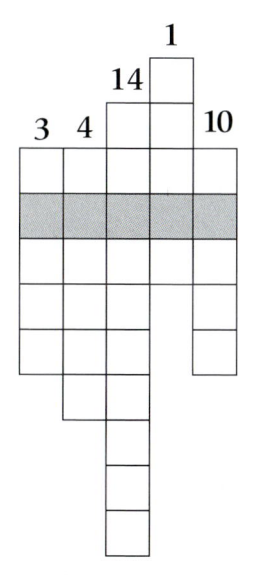

My _ _ _ _ _ has got a big garden.

In the house

The family

1 Look at Elaine's family tree and do the crossword.

1. Albert is Elaine's…
2. Adrian and Patricia are Elaine's …
3. Harry, Elaine, Patricia and Adrian are Albert's …
4. David is Elaine's …
5. Harry is Susan's …
6. Elaine is Harry's …
7. Patricia is Steven's …
8. Steven is Elaine's …
9. Mary and Steven are Patricia's …
10. Elaine is Elizabeth's …
11. Patricia and Adrian are Mary and Steven's…
12. Steven is Mary's …
13. Elizabeth and Albert are Adrian's …
14. Susan is Harry's …
15. Adrian is Patricia's …
16. Elizabeth is Elaine's …
17. Harry is Albert's …
18. Mary is Elaine's …
19. Susan is David's …
20. Harry is Mary's …
21. Elaine is Mary's …

The family

11

2 Make pairs.

1. mother   wife
2. grandfather   uncle
3. sister   daughter
4. son   father
5. aunt   niece
6. husband   grandmother
7. nephew   brother

3 Look at the pictures and complete the sentences.

father - husband - daughter - children - sister - brothers

1. Julie and Tom are married and they have a ....

2. Michelle's .... buys her a lot of sweets.

3. Mr and Mrs Brand have got three ....

4. Barbara's .... is very tall.

5. Mary has got three ....

6. Victor is playing with his little ....

4 Who are the people at Fred and Susie's wedding? Find seven words in the wordsearch box, then complete the sentence with the remaining letters.

B	R	A	U	N	T	E	L
R	F	A	T	H	E	R	C
O	A	T	I	V	E	S	O
T	M	O	T	H	E	R	U
H	F	U	N	C	L	E	S
E	R	I	E	N	D	S	I
R	S	I	S	T	E	R	N

There are a lot of

_ _ _ _ _ _ _ _ _*

and _ _ _ _ _ _ _

at the wedding.

*People from the same family.

5 Do the crossword, then complete the sentence with the letters in the grey squares.

1. Another word for "mum".
2. Another word for "dad".
3. The man I married.
4. A boy who has the same parents as me.
5. My daughter's daughter.
6. The woman I married.

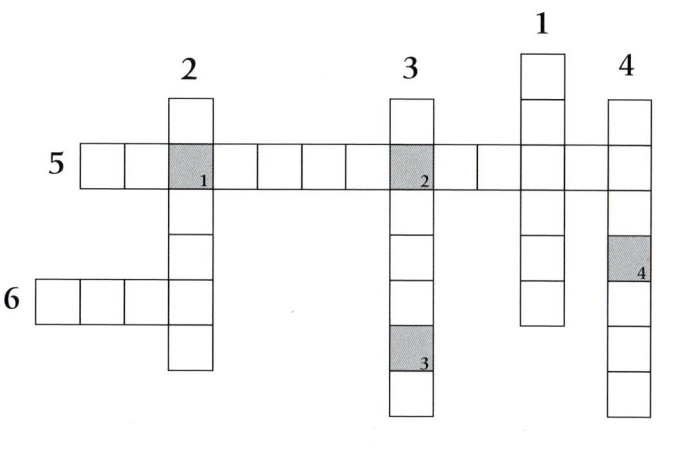

My mother's sister is my _ _ _ _.
                               1 2 3 4

The family

13

grammar

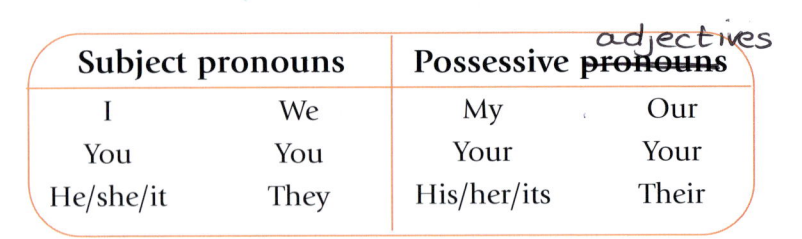

Subject pronouns		Possessive ~~pronouns~~ adjectives	
I	We	My	Our
You	You	Your	Your
He/she/it	They	His/her/its	Their

6 Look at Elaine's family tree and complete the sentences.

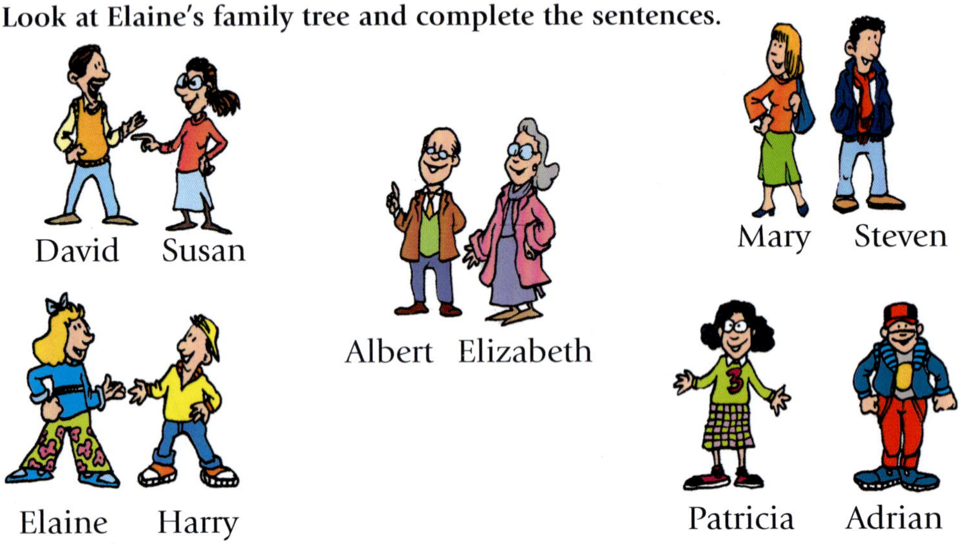

David   Susan

Albert   Elizabeth

Mary   Steven

Elaine   Harry

Patricia   Adrian

Harry is Elaine's brother. ⟶ *He is her brother.*

1. Elizabeth is Susan's mother.
   She is .... mother.

2. Albert is Susan's father.
   .... is her father.

3. Albert and Elizabeth are Adrian's grandparents. .... are .... grandparents.

4. Susan is Elaine and Harry's mother. .... is .... mother.

5. Mary is Steven's wife.
   .... is .... wife.

6. David is Susan's husband.
   .... is .... husband.

7. Patricia and Adrian are Albert's grandchildren.
   .... are .... grandchildren.

8. Adrian is Harry's cousin.
   .... is .... cousin.

9. David is Patricia's uncle.
   .... is .... uncle.

10. Mary is Elaine's aunt.
    .... is .... aunt.

7 Put in the correct ~~pronoun~~ adjective.

1. My grandfather is reading .... newspaper.

2. She is riding .... bike.

3. They are walking .... dog.

4. The girls are playing with .... dolls.

5. She is driving .... car.

6. He's having .... breakfast.

Now describe your family.

Parts of the body

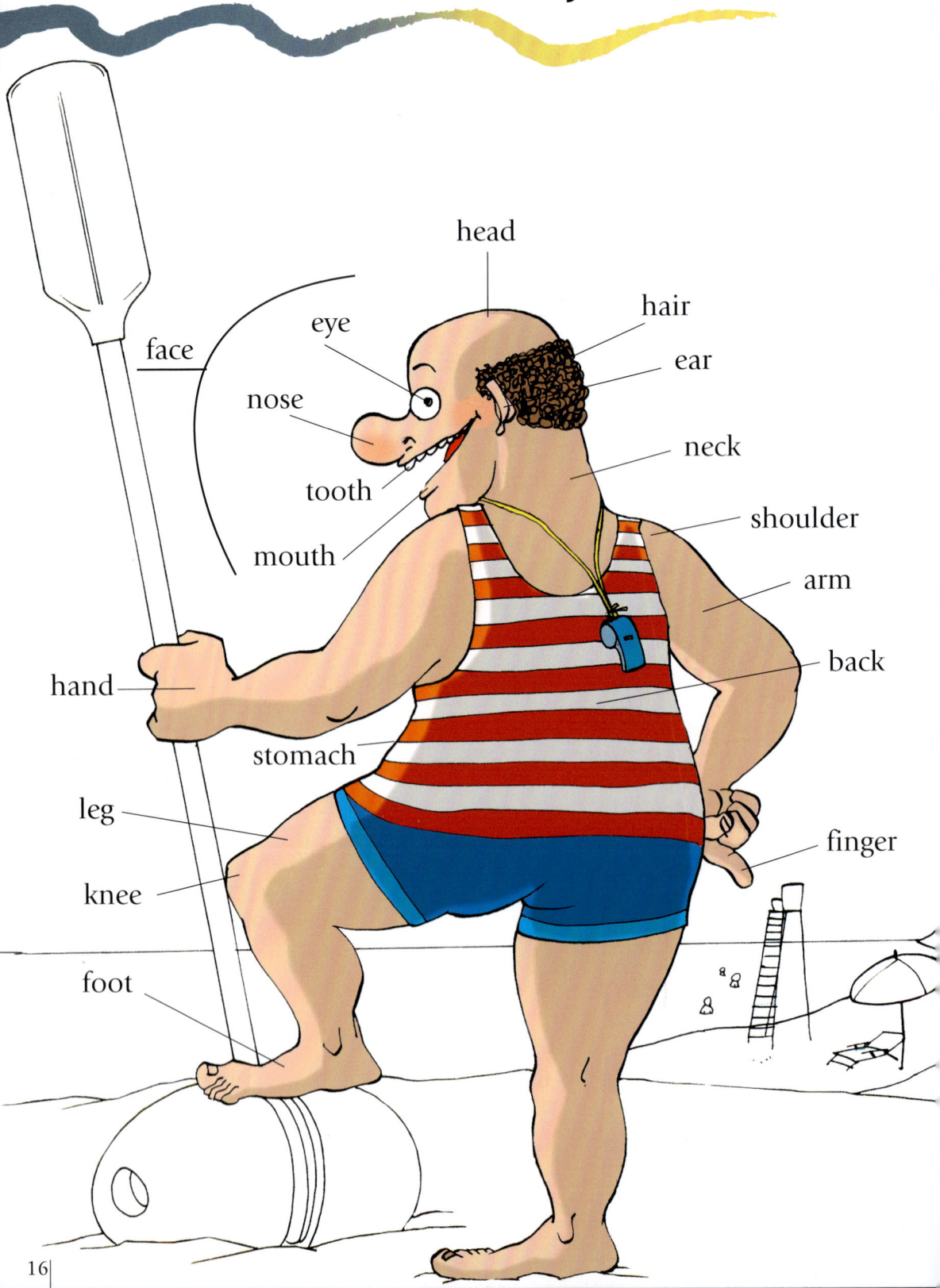

head
hair
eye
ear
face
nose
neck
tooth
shoulder
mouth
arm
back
hand
stomach
leg
finger
knee
foot

16

1 Which part of the body is missing? Look at the pictures and write the word.

_ _ G _

_ _ A _

A _ _

_ _ N _

_ O _ _

2 Look at the pictures and complete the sentences.

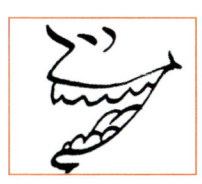

1. You use it for talking.
....

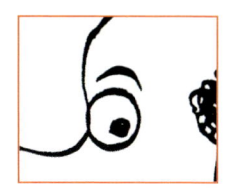

2. You use them for looking at things.
....

3. You use them for listening.
....

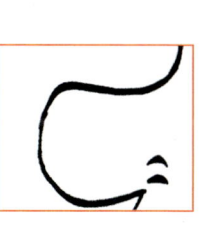

4. You use this for smelling things.
....

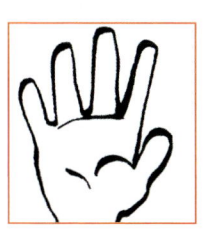

5. You use this for touching things.
....

3 Do the crossword.

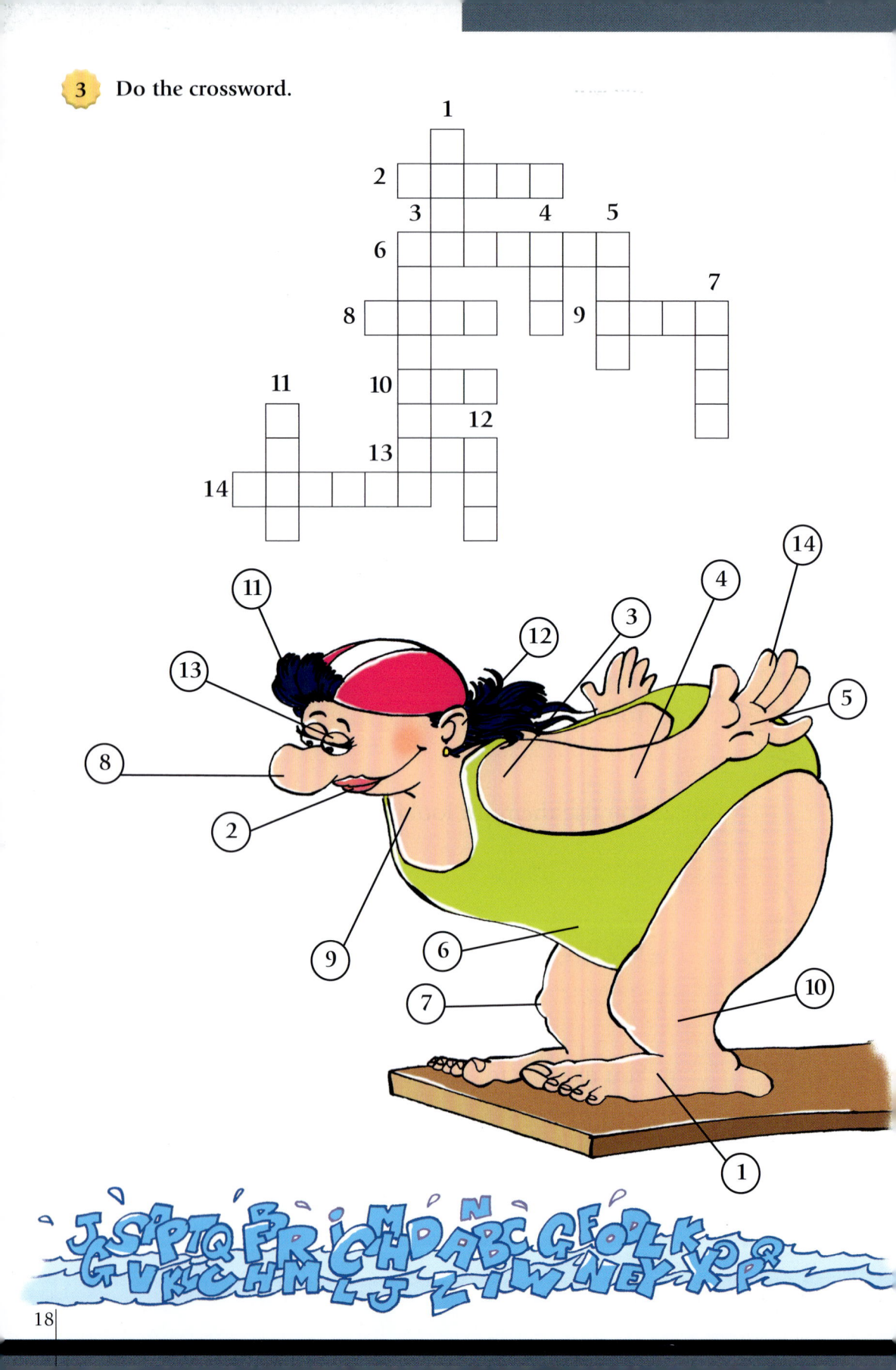

4 Find four words in the wordsearch box to complete the sentences and use the remaining letters to form a question. Put the letters in the correct order to complete the other sentences.

S T O M A C H
W H E R E D E
B A C K O E A
S T O O T H D
I T H U R T ?

_ _ _ _ _   _ _ _ _
_ _   _ _ _ _   _

1. My .... hurts.
   I've got a ....
   E H C A D A E H .

2. My .... hurts.
   I've got ....
   C K B A H C A E .

3. My .... hurts.
   I've got ....
   H C A M T S O H E C A .

4. My .... hurts.
   I've got ....
   H E C A T T H O O .

5 Do the crossword.

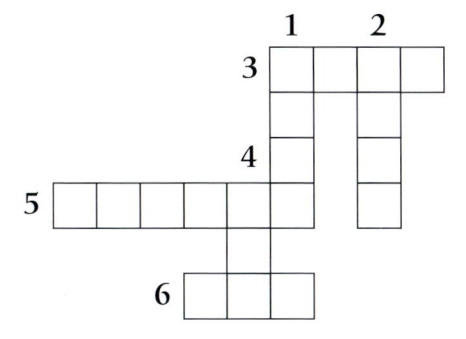

1. My brother has got purple ... .
2. He has got a ring in his ... .
3. He has a scar on his right ... .
4. He's wearing a lot of earrings in his left ... .
5. He's got a big ring on his ... .
6. He's got a tattoo on his ... .

Parts of the body

19

grammar

Plurals

To form the plural of most English nouns, you add an "s" to the noun.
For example :   hand / **hands**

But some nouns have irregular plurals, for example:
foot / **feet**
tooth / **teeth**

6 Find the plural nouns in the wordsearch box and then complete the sentence with the remaining letters.

F	I	N	G	E	R	S
M	H	E	A	D	S	T
O	P	A	R	M	S	E
U	L	E	G	S	A	E
T	R	T	S	O	F	T
H	F	E	E	T	T	H
S	H	E	B	O	D	Y

The title of this unit is:

....

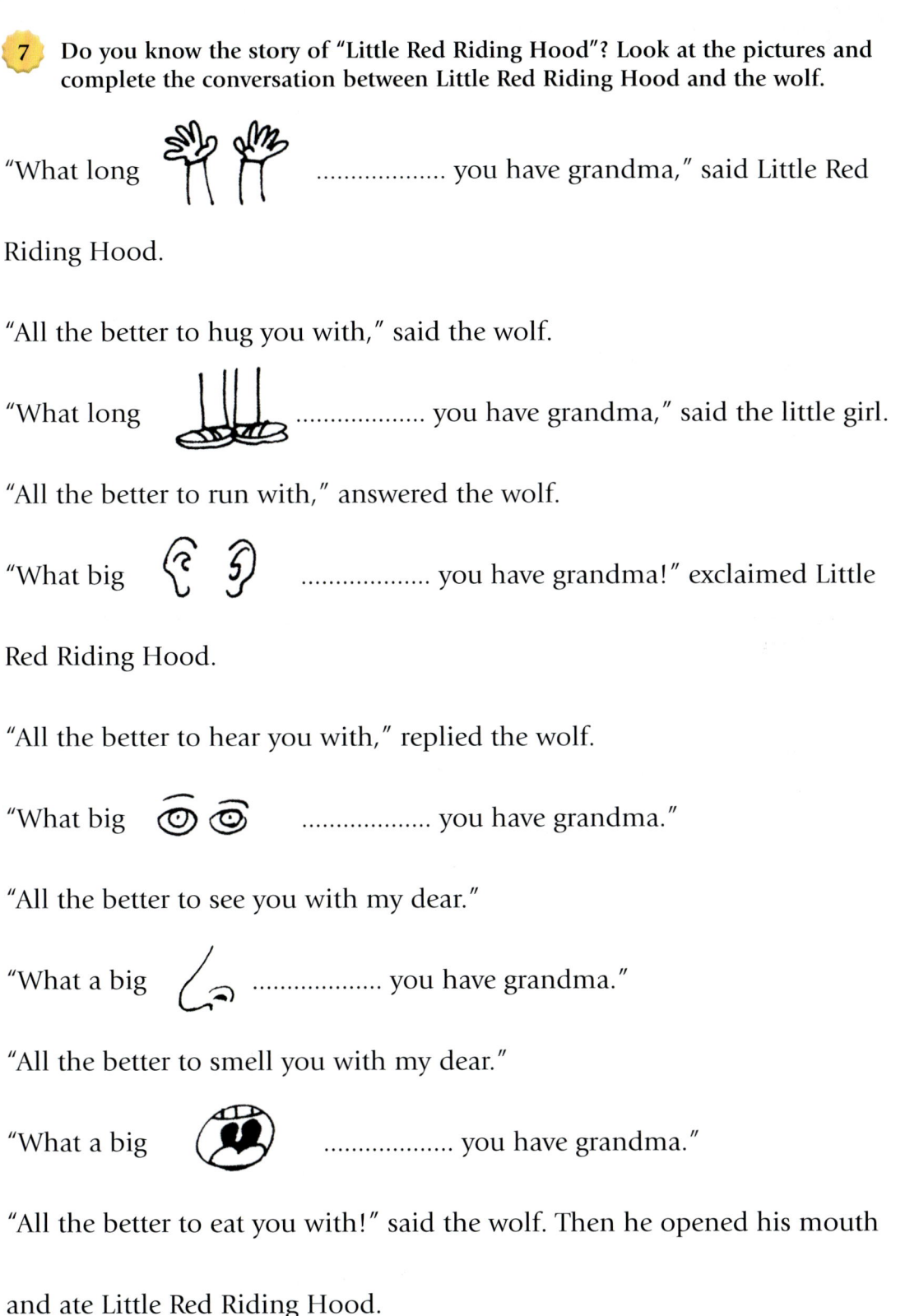

7 Do you know the story of "Little Red Riding Hood"? Look at the pictures and complete the conversation between Little Red Riding Hood and the wolf.

"What long ………………… you have grandma," said Little Red Riding Hood.

"All the better to hug you with," said the wolf.

"What long ………………… you have grandma," said the little girl.

"All the better to run with," answered the wolf.

"What big ………………… you have grandma!" exclaimed Little Red Riding Hood.

"All the better to hear you with," replied the wolf.

"What big ………………… you have grandma."

"All the better to see you with my dear."

"What a big ………………… you have grandma."

"All the better to smell you with my dear."

"What a big ………………… you have grandma."

"All the better to eat you with!" said the wolf. Then he opened his mouth and ate Little Red Riding Hood.

Parts of the body

21

Colours

white

black

red

blue

yellow

green

brown

grey

pink

orange

purple

beige

1 Look at the pictures and complete the colours.

milk ....

ink ....

a tomato ....

the sea ....

a lemon ....

grass ....

a chestnut ....

a mouse ....

an orange ....

a pig ....

a cloak ....

Colours

23

2 Find the names of twelve colours in the wordsearch box and then complete the question with the remaining letters. →↑

O	R	A	N	G	E	H	A	V
B	P	E	Y	R	O	R	E	D
R	I	U	B	E	I	G	E	G
O	N	O	L	Y	T	B	A	G
W	K	P	U	R	P	L	E	R
N	G	R	E	E	E	A	N	E
W	H	I	T	E	P	C	E	E
Y	E	L	L	O	W	K	N	N

_ _ _ _ _ _ _
_ _ _ _ _
_ _ _ _ _ _ _ _ _ _ ?

3 Do the crossword, then complete the sentence with the letters in the grey squares.

1. The colour of pigs.
2. The colour of oranges.
3. The colour of snow.
4. The colour of ink.
5. The colour of tomatoes.
6. The colour of lemons.

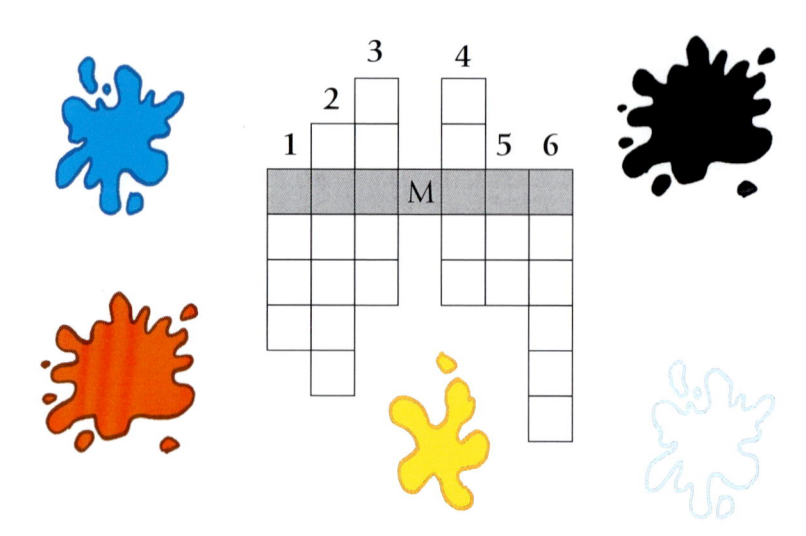

Yellow, blue and red are _ _ _ M _ _ _ colours. If you mix them, you can obtain other colours, for example: green, purple and orange.

24

4 Can you remember the colours of the rainbow? Write them in the squares.

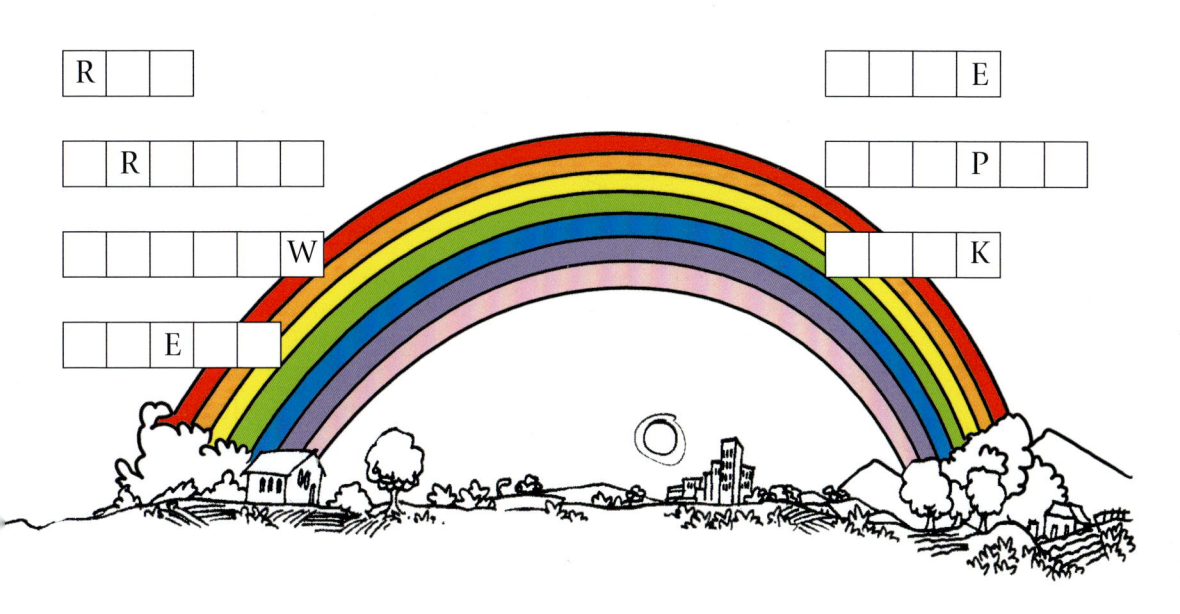

| R | | |

| | R | | | |

| | | | W | |

| | E | | |

| | | | E |

| | | | P | |

| | | K |

5 What colour are these flags?

The British flag is ....
and ....

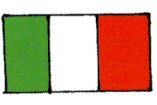

The Italian flag is .... and ....

The French flag is ....and ....

The German flag is ....and ....

The Spanish flag has two .... stripes
and one .... stripe.

The Swiss flag is .... with a .... cross.

6 Elaine and her family are describing their favourite colours.
Read the description and write the colour.

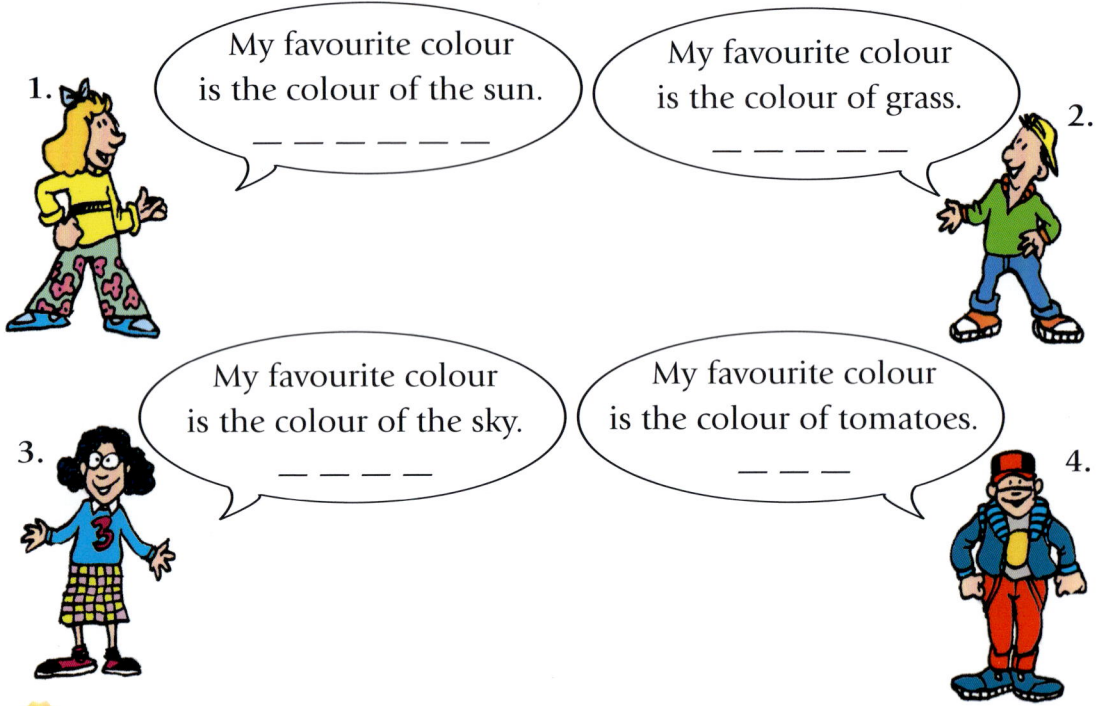

1. My favourite colour is the colour of the sun.
_ _ _ _ _ _

2. My favourite colour is the colour of grass.
_ _ _ _ _

3. My favourite colour is the colour of the sky.
_ _ _ _

4. My favourite colour is the colour of tomatoes.
_ _ _

7 Complete the sentences to describe the house.

1. The roof is ....
2. The chimney is ....
3. The walls are ....
4. The door is ....
5. The windows are ....
6. The garage is ....

grammar

> **Adjectives in English *always* come before the noun.**
>
> Eg. My brother has got a **red** car.
>
> Which pen do you want?
> The **blue** one.

8 Complete the sentences with the colours below.

Claire has got ▢ .... eyes.

Bananas are ▢ ....

Spinach is ▢ ....

Cherries are ▢ ....

Pigs are ▢ ....

She's got long, ▢ .... hair.

Look at those beautiful ▢ .... clouds.

Diane has got a new ▢ .... dress.

There is a ▢ .... panther at the zoo.

The sky is ▢ ...., it's going to rain.

grey   purple   black   brown   green
  yellow   white   pink   red   blue

Colours

27

Food and drink

water	wine	coffee	milk
tea	bread	soup	rice
sausages	chicken	meat	fish
cheese	vegetables	fruit	eggs
pizza	ice cream	butter	

1 Find five words in the wordsearch box and then complete the sentence with the remaining letters.

```
C O F F E E W
D R T E A I I
N W A T E R N
M I L K K S E
```

They are all _ _ _ _ _ _ _ .

2 Look at the pictures and do the crossword. Complete the sentence with the letters in the grey squares.

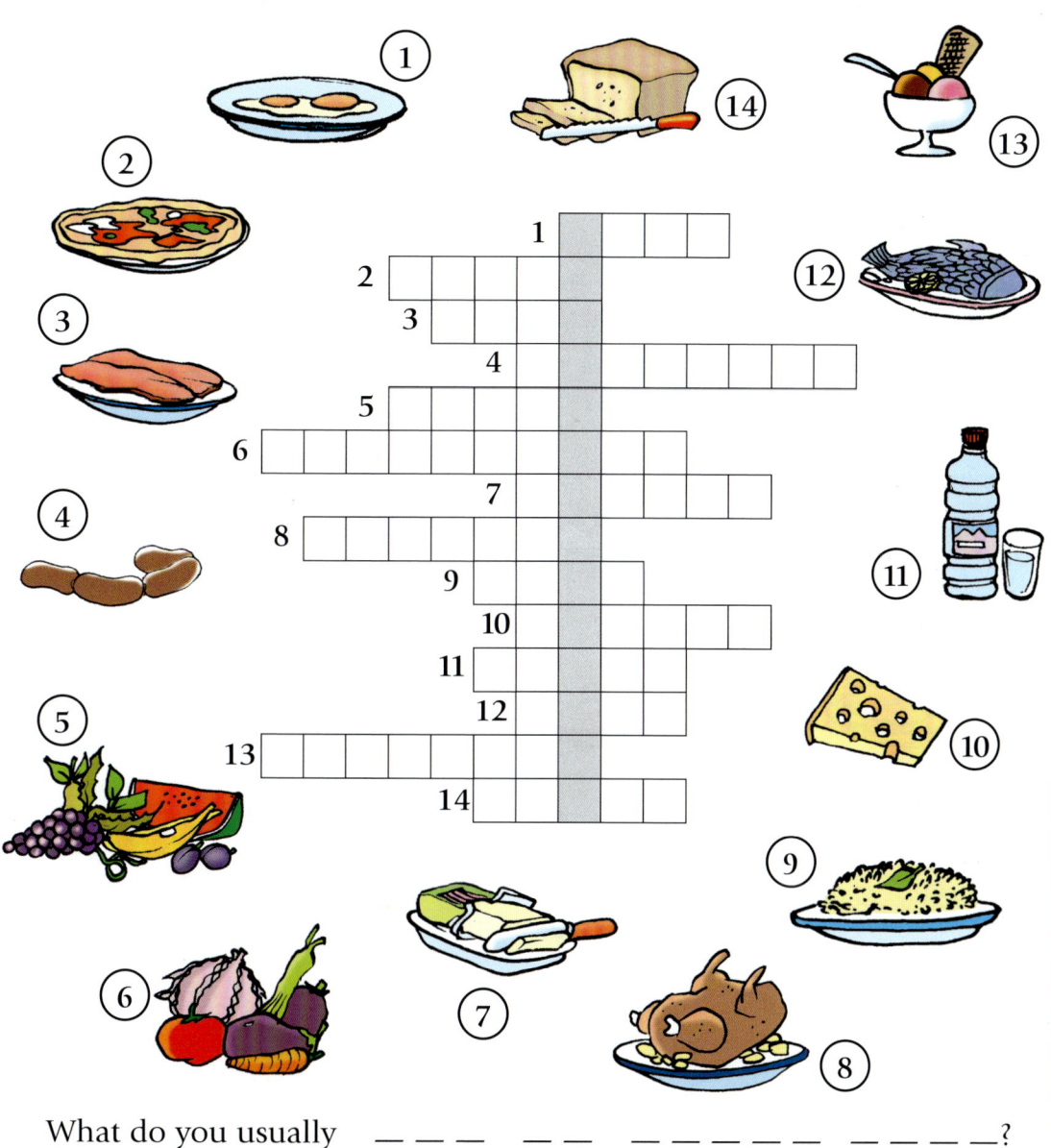

What do you usually _ _ _   _ _   _ _ _ _ _ _   _ _ _ _ ?

Food and drink

29

3 Do the crossword.

4 What is Mrs Brown buying?

7. ....
3. ....
5. ....
8. ....
9. ....
2. ....
10. ....
4. ....
1. ....
6. ....

5 Put the words from exercise 4 into the correct squares.
Complete the sentence with the letters in the grey squares.

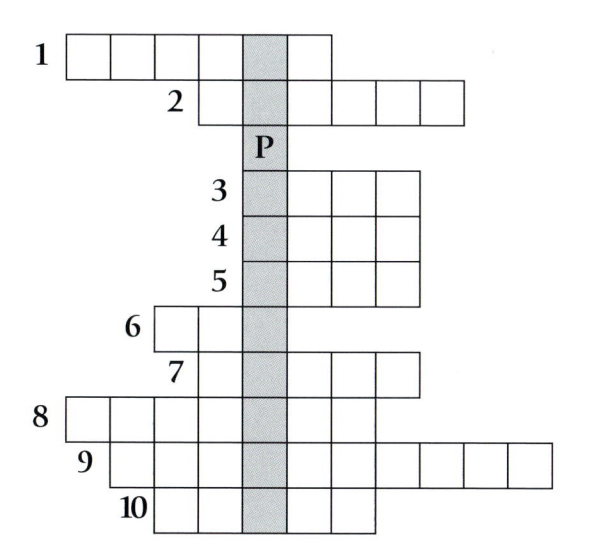

1
2
P
3
4
5
6
7
8
9
10

Mrs Brown is doing the shopping at the __ __ P _ _ _ _ _ _ _ _ _ .

Food and drink

31

6 Look at the pictures and complete the sentences.

1. Bill likes eating cheese with a glass of red ....

2. Fred eats a lot of ....

3. Fiona loves ....

4. Martha likes .... with a cup of tea.

5. Mike often eats ....

6. Carol is thirsty, she wants some ....

grammar

I like pasta a lot.
She likes chocolate.
He quite likes vegetables.

She doesn't like fish much.
We don't like eggs.
They don't like pizza at all.

7 Right or wrong? Find the mistakes and correct the sentences.

                                right wrong

1. I don't like beer much. ☐ ☐ ....
2. She likes fish quite. ☐ ☐ ....
3. He doesn't like coffee a lot. ☐ ☐ ....
4. We like ice cream a lot. ☐ ☐ ....
5. They like milk at all. ☐ ☐ ....
6. She quite likes eggs. ☐ ☐ ....
7. I don't like sausages at all. ☐ ☐ ....

8 Complete the sentences with the correct form of "like" and the word represented by the picture.

1. Sheena .... _ _ _ _ .

2. I .... _ _ _ a lot.

3. Paul .... _ _ _ _ _ _ at all.

4. They quite .... _ _ _ _ _ .

5. I .... _ _ _ _ much.

6. We both quite .... _ _ _ _ _ _ _ _ _ _ .

7. Janet .... _ _ _ _ _ _ at all.

8. They .... _ _ _ _ a lot.

What do you like?
What don't you like?

Food and drink

33

Clothes

skirt	trousers	sweater	T-shirt
shoes	socks	shirt	blouse
jacket	dress	jeans	sweatshirt
anorak	coat	raincoat	tie
vest	pants	pyjamas	

1 Do the crossword.

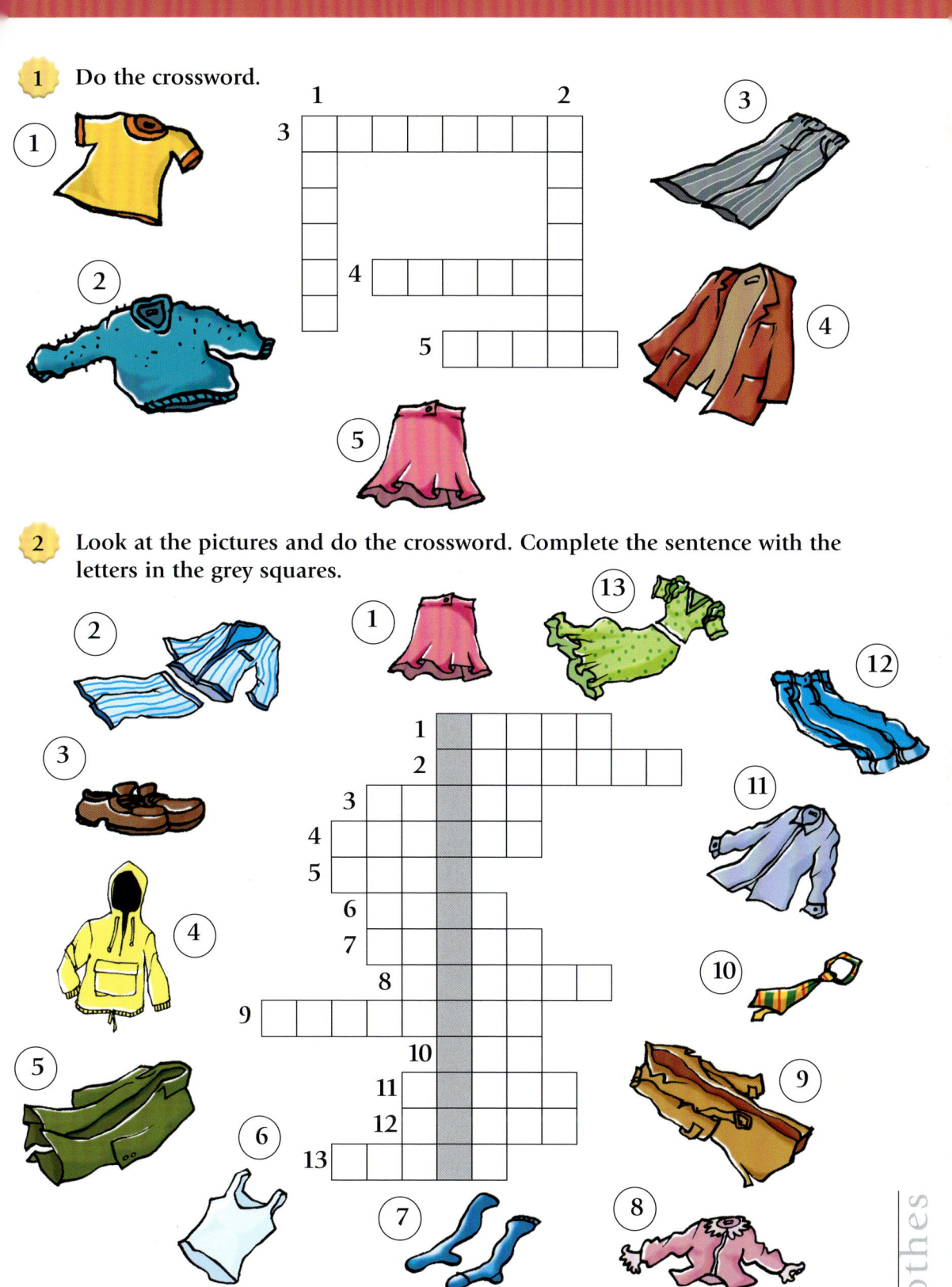

2 Look at the pictures and do the crossword. Complete the sentence with the letters in the grey squares.

I like _ _ _ _ _ _   _ _ _ _ _ _ _ .

Clothes

35

3 Find nineteen articles of clothing in the wordsearch box and use the remaining letters to complete the conversation.

```
P Y J A M A S C O A T
S O C K S S D S A R B
W I V S S H R H N A L
E T E H K I E O O I O
A E S R I R S E R N U
T E T A R T S S A C S
S W E A T E R J K O E
H T S H I R T E G A T
I R P A N T S A E T I
R J A C K E T N E N E
T R O U S E R S O N E
```

Sarah is buying a new sweater. She's in a clothes shop...
Shop assistant: *Do you like this one?*
Sarah: *Yes! But I don't like the colour very much...*
__ __ _____ __ _____ ___?
Shop assistant: *Yes, here it is.*

4 Make words with the letters and fill in the blanks.

A ERITIHTS

1. You put this around your neck when you are wearing a shirt.
   It's a ....
2. You often wear this under a jacket with or without a tie.
   It's a ....

B EULKSRTIBOS

3. It can be long, short or mini! It's a ....
4. A shirt is for a man and a .... is for a woman.

5 What is Gillian putting in her suitcase? Write the words in the correct spaces. Complete the sentence with the letters in the grey squares.

1. ☐☐☐▨
2. ☐☐☐▨☐
3. ☐▨☐☐
4. ☐☐☐☐▨☐
5. ☐☐☐☐▨
6. ☐☐▨☐☐
7. ☐☐☐☐▨☐
8. ▨☐☐☐☐☐☐

Gillian likes wearing _ _ _ _ _ _ _ _ .

6 What is Gary putting in his suitcase? Write the words in the correct spaces. Complete the sentence with the letters in the grey squares.

1. ☐☐☐☐▨   4. ☐☐▨
2. ☐▨☐☐☐   5. ▨☐☐☐☐
3. ☐▨☐☐

Gary likes wearing comfortable _ _ _ _ _ _ .

Clothes

37

7 Look at the pictures and complete the sentences.

1. Put your .... on!

2. It's raining, put your .... on.

3. Put this .... on, it's nice.

4. It's cold today, don't go out with only a .... on.

5. I'm hot, I'll take off my ....

6. These .... are too big.

7. You're still in your .... !

8. Are you going out without your .... ?

8 Put the words from exercise 7 into the correct squares.
Complete the sentence with the letters in the grey squares.

Another way of saying "put on your clothes": G_ _ _ _ _ _ _ _D.

grammar

I'm putting on my clothes…

I'm putting on my dress.

You're putting on your sweater.

He's putting on his shirt.

We're putting on our socks.

You're putting on your shoes.

They're putting on their coats.

9 The opposite of "putting on" is "taking off". Make the same sentences, using "taking off".

I'm taking off my dress.

....

....

....

....

....

Animals

dog　　　cat　　　cow　　　horse

pig　　　hen　　　rabbit　　　cockerel

lion　　　fish　　　bird　　　monkey

sheep　　　donkey　　　crocodile　　　bear

giraffe　　　elephant　　　snake

1 Which animals live on a farm? Tick the correct box.

	yes	no		yes	no
cat	☐	☐	rabbit	☐	☐
crocodile	☐	☐	giraffe	☐	☐
dog	☐	☐	sheep	☐	☐
cow	☐	☐	monkey	☐	☐
lion	☐	☐	donkey	☐	☐
horse	☐	☐	hen	☐	☐
elephant	☐	☐	snake	☐	☐
pig	☐	☐	cockerel	☐	☐

2 You're at the zoo. Where are the animals? Put the correct number in each circle.

① snakes
② elephants
③ bears
④ lions
⑤ giraffes
⑥ crocodiles
⑦ monkeys

a. b. c. d. e. f. g.

Animals

41

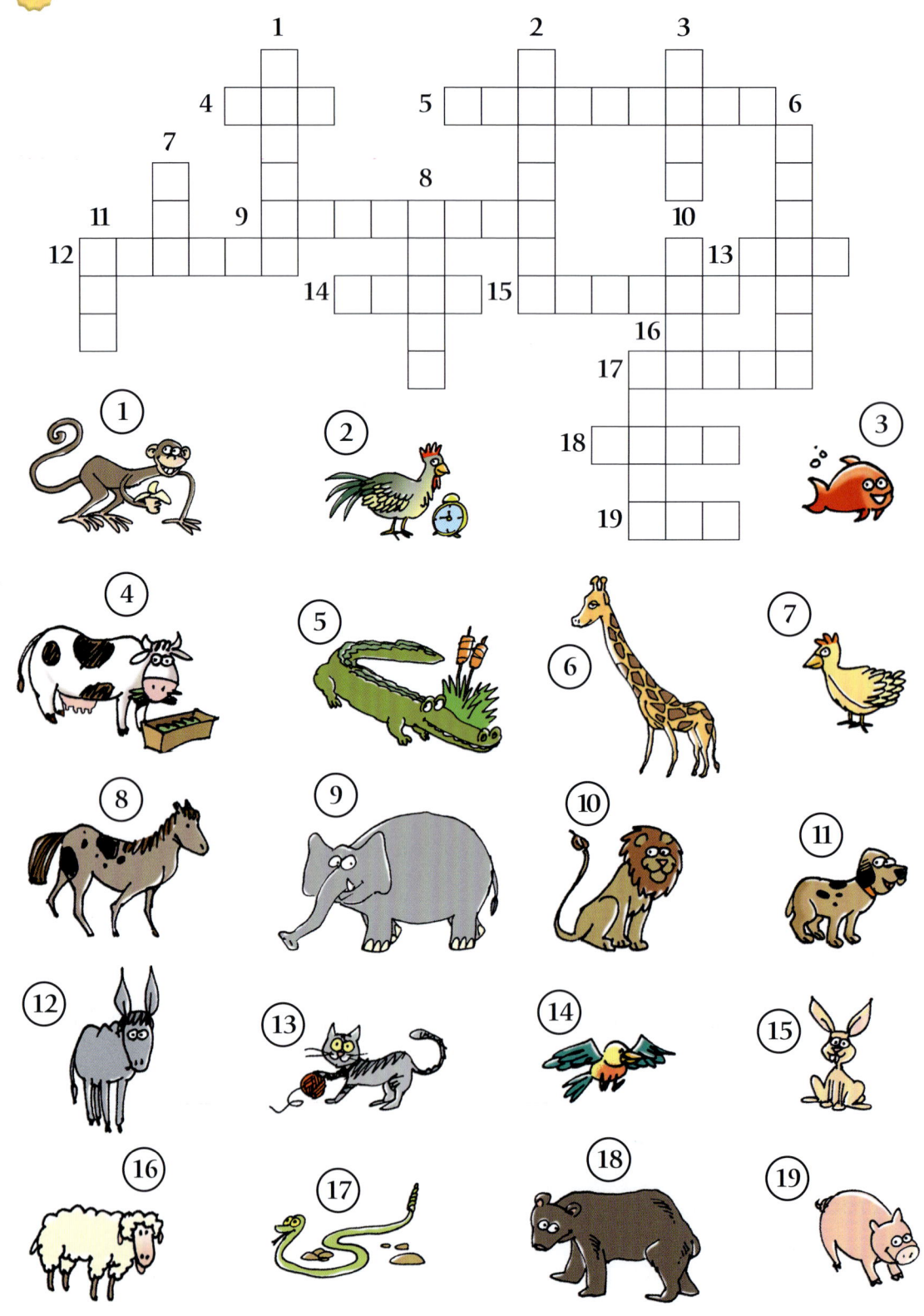

3 Do the crossword.

4 Find seven animals in the wordsearch box.
The remaining letters form the name of a pet.

```
H O R S E C F C
H E N P I G I O
R A B B I T S W
S H E E P A H T
```

_ _ _

5 Read the sentences and do the crossword.

1. This animal has a very long neck.
2. This is a domestic animal.
3. This animal is friendly and faithful.
4. This animal gives us milk.
5. This animal likes carrots.
6. This animal wakes everyone up in the morning.
7. This animal lays eggs.
8. This animal is covered in wool.
9. This animal can fly.
10. This animal swims in water.
11. This animal is long, thin, and has no legs.
12. This farm animal is short, fat and pink.

Animals

43

6 Here are some expressions with animals. Write the name of the animal.

She swims like a …!	HFSI	= She swims very well.
	....	
He eats like a …!	REHSO	= He eats a lot.
	....	
He is the black... of the family!	PEHSE	= He isn't accepted by his family
	....	
It's a ...'s life!	DGO	= Life is difficult.
	....	
She's crying ... tears!	OCCRLEIOD	= She's not sincere.
	....	

7 Put the letters in the correct order to complete the story.

A farmer wants to sell his (WOC) ...., so he goes to the market on his (RESHO) ....
At the market he sells his (OWC) .... and buys a (ENH) ...., but the (NEH) .... doesn't like the farmer and it runs away. The farmer buys a nice little (gip)........................... instead. He wins a (SHIF) .... playing bingo, then goes home on his (RSEHO) ...., with the (GPI) .... under his arm and the (SHIF) .... in a bag.

44

grammar

Comparative adjectives

In English we add "er" to adjectives to form comparative adjectives. When the adjective has two or more syllables, we put "more" in front of the adjective.

Rabbits are small**er** than elephants.

Giraffes have long**er** necks than horses.

Dogs are **more** faithful than cats.

8 Put the words in the correct order and write the sentences.

1. donkey – more – rabbit. – is – A – stubborn – than – a

....

2. taller – a – than – monkey. – A – is – giraffe

....

3. hen. – than – more – monkey – A – is – intelligent – a

....

4. A – cow. – sheep – a – smaller – is – than

....

5. dangerous – rooster. – a – bear – more – than – is – A

....

6. faster – than – horse – can – A – run – donkey. – a

....

7. than – lion – cat. – ferocious – A – a – is – more

....

8. a - crocodile – slower – is – than - A – rabbit.

....

Do you like animals?
Have you got any pets?

Nature

tree

flower

sea

mountains

country

sky

field

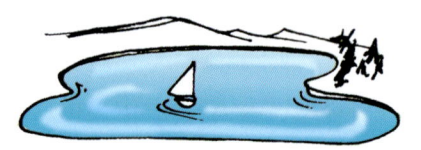

lake

river

sun

star

moon

woods

hills

island

1 Do the crossword.

2 Find fifteen words in the wordsearch box and make a sentence with the remaining letters.

```
M O U N T A I N S F S
I S L A N D S K Y L T
M O O N L A K E N O A
O M O T R I V E R W R
S U N R R E S E A E P
O L L E F I E L D R U
T I O E C O U N T R Y
H I L L S N W O O D S
```

_ _   _ _ _ _

_ _ _ _ _ _ _ _ _ !

Nature

3 Look at the picture and write the words you know.

....

....

....

....

4 The picture in exercise 3 shows the countryside during the day.
What can you see in the sky at night-time?

I can see the _ _ _ _ and the _ _ _ _ _ _.

5 What do you know about Great Britain? Complete the sentences.

1. .... Windermere is in the Lake District.

2. Ireland is an ....

3. The Thames is a .... which runs through London.

4. Ben Nevis is the highest .... in Great Britain.

6 Look at the pictures and complete the sentences.

1. There is a beautiful pink .... in my garden.

2. There is an apple .... in my garden.

3. Mark goes skiing in the .... in the winter.

4. Gary and Paul are in the .... looking for mushrooms.

5. Mr and Mrs Higgins have got a cottage in the ....

6. Robert likes walking in the ....

7 Put the words into the correct spaces.

fields – moon – sun – stars – sky – flowers

In the summer the .... shines, the .... is blue, the .... are green and gardens are full of colourful .... At night the pale .... comes out and the .... sparkle in the dark blue sky.

Nature

8 What can you see from the windows?

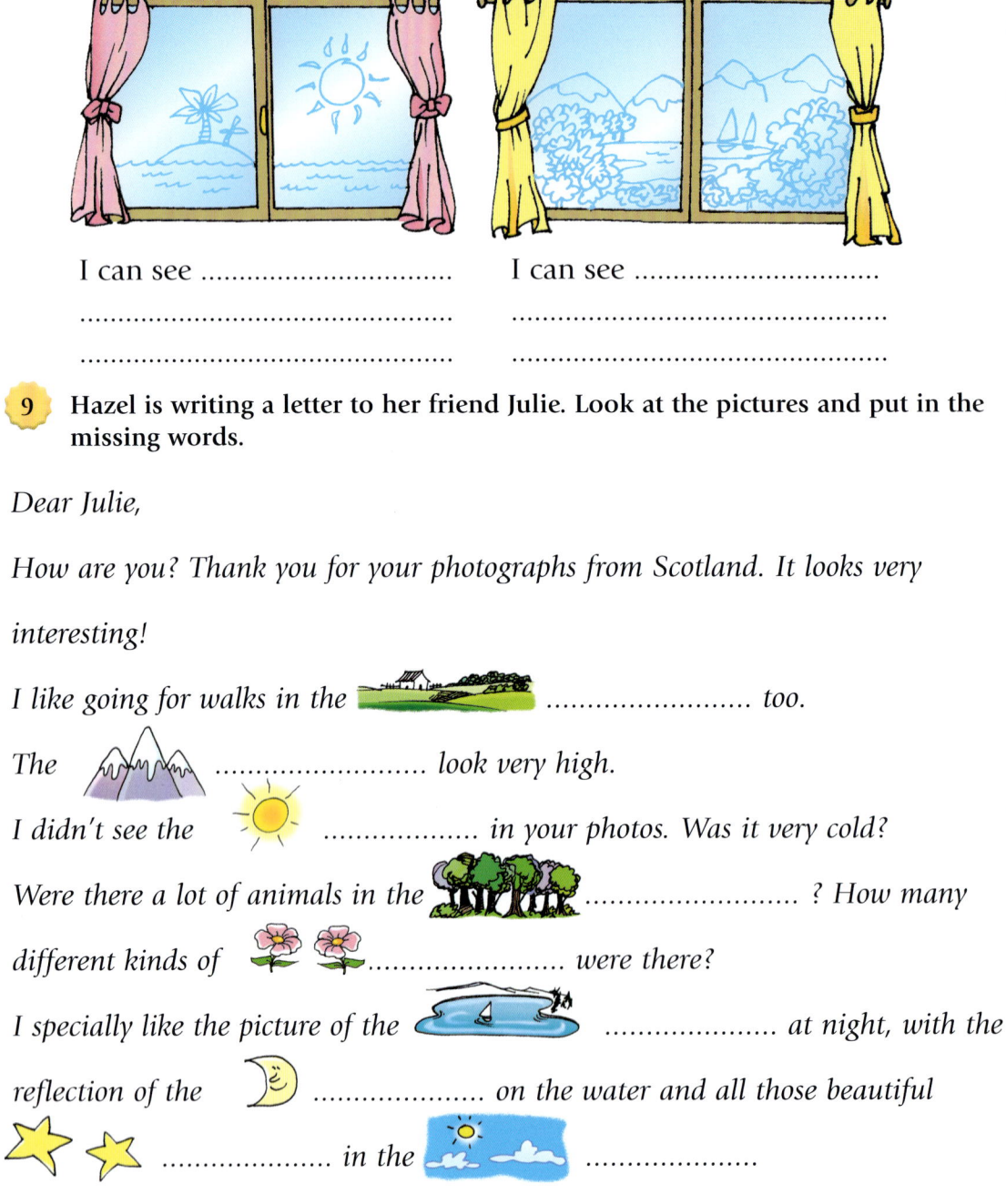

I can see ....

I can see ....

9 Hazel is writing a letter to her friend Julie. Look at the pictures and put in the missing words.

Dear Julie,

How are you? Thank you for your photographs from Scotland. It looks very interesting!

I like going for walks in the .... too.

The .... look very high.

I didn't see the .... in your photos. Was it very cold?

Were there a lot of animals in the .... ? How many different kinds of .... were there?

I specially like the picture of the .... at night, with the reflection of the .... on the water and all those beautiful .... in the ....

The next time I go on a trip, I'll send you some photos.

Love,
Hazel

grammar

*The verbs **can** and **want** are irregular. **Can** is always followed by the infinitive of another verb, without "**to**"*

eg. I can **see** the mountains.
     I can **swim** in the sea.
     I can't **swim** in the lake.

***Want** can also be followed by another verb, but the verb uses the infinitive with "**to**"*

eg. I want **to go** for a walk beside the lake.
     Do you want **to sit** in the sun?
     I don't want **to climb** the mountains.

10 Look at the pictures and complete the sentences using can or want.

1. Look, it's dark outside. .... you see the .... ?

2. Do you .... to go for a walk in the .... ?

3. John .... see the .... from his window.

4. .... they swim in the .... ? No, it's too cold!

5. We don't .... to climb the ....

Do you like living in the country?
Would you like to live in the country?

Nature

51

At school

| classroom |  blackboard |  desk |  chair |

| bin |  backpack |  diary |  pencil case |

| exercise book |  book |  pencil |  pen |

| eraser/ rubber |  pencil sharpener |  felt pen | 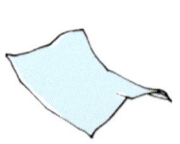 paper |

| sticky tape |  ruler |  glue stick |  scissors |

1 Look at the picture and write the words.

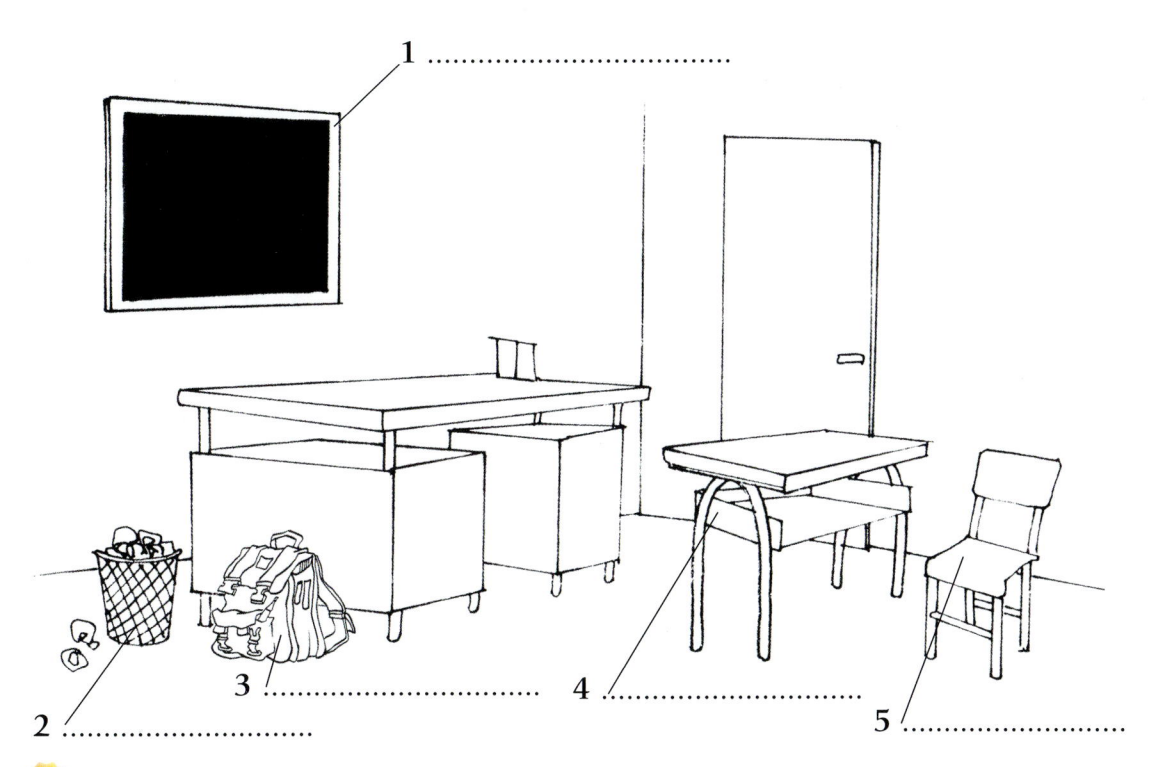

1 ....
2 ....
3 ....
4 ....
5 ....

2 Do the crossword. Complete the question with the letters in the grey squares.

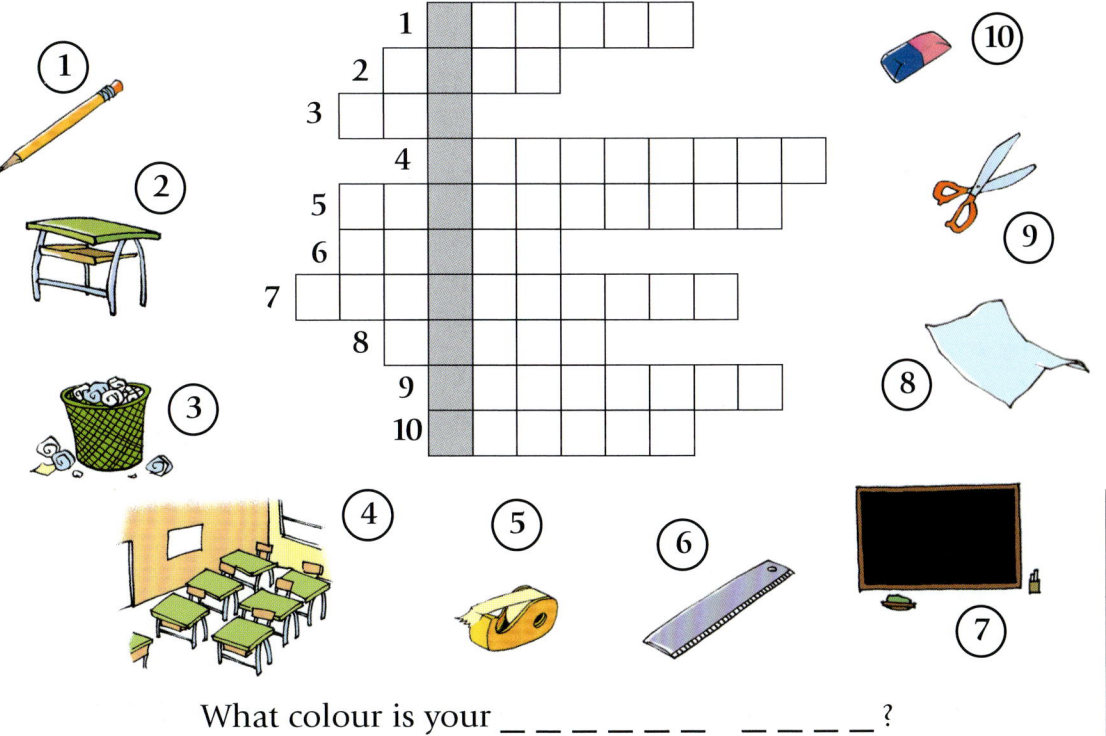

What colour is your _ _ _ _ _ _ _ _ _ _ ?

At school

53

3 Write the words.

3 ....
4 ....
5 ....
6 ....
7 ....
8 ....
1 ....
2 ....

4 Find eighteen ~~18~~ words in the wordsearch box. The remaining letters form a question.

```
B L A C K B O A R D D P
B A C K P A C K B I N E
C D E S K D I A R Y G N
L F O P A P E R Y P L C
A E O E R A S E R E U I
S L U E N J O Y G N E L
S T I C K Y T A P E S C
R P E N C I L O I N T A
O E S C I S S O R S I S
O N R U L E R G T O C E
M S C B O O K H O O K L
E X E R C I S E B O O K
```

_ _   _ _ _   _ _ _ _ _   _ _ _ _ _   _ _   _ _ _ _ _ _ ?

54

5 Look at the pictures and complete the sentences.

1. The teacher is writing on the ....

2. Lisa is colouring her picture with ....

3. Paul is reading his ....

4. The pupils are already in the ....

6 What is it? Put the letters in the correct order and write the words.

1. You use this to write.   N P E   ....

2. You use this to erase mistakes.   R S E E A R   ....

3. You use this to sharpen pencils.   CLPIEN HSRPANERE   ....

4. You use this to draw straight lines.   R L R U E   ....

5. You use these to cut.   C S S S I R O S   ....

7 Match the objects with the sentences.

1. Mr Watson is reading
2. Emma is writing a letter on
3. He is throwing the paper in the
4. Martin is putting his book in his

a. a sheet of coloured paper.
b. backpack.
c. a book.
d. bin.

At school

55

8 Do the crossword.

1. The teacher writes on this.
2. You use this to write and draw.
3. You use this to glue things together.
4. You use these to cut.
5. This is the place where you have your lessons.
6. You use this to erase mistakes.
7. A student's table.
8. You keep your pens, pencils and other writing things in this.
9. You write and draw on this.
10. You use this to draw straight lines.

grammar

*The imperative form of the verb is used to give orders and commands. To form the imperative, use the **infinitive without "to"**.*

Listen to the teacher.
Repeat after me!
Finish the exercises.
Be quiet!

*The negative form of the imperative uses **don't + infinitive***

Don't walk on the grass.
Don't touch the picture.

*The first person plural or "we" form takes **let's + infinitive***

Let's go to school.
Let's have lunch at one o'clock.

9 Put the correct form of the imperative into the spaces.

1. .... so loud, I can't concentrate. *(talk)*

2. .... your books at page ten. *(open)*

3. .... it on my desk with the other exercise books. *(put)*

4. .... on the desk, it's wet! *(sit)*

5. "What shall we do after school?" "........................ to the park." *(go)*

6. .... to this cd, the music's great! *(listen)*

7. .... your name at the top of the page. *(write)*

8. .... a party on Saturday, it's my birthday! *(have)*

Jobs

teacher

office worker

factory worker

architect

farmer

waiter

shop assistant

doctor

mechanic

policeman

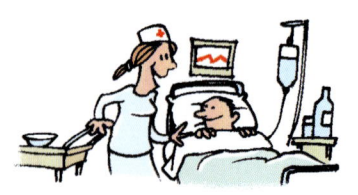

nurse

electrician

bricklayer

chef

journalist

lawyer

actor

1 Match the jobs with the correct place of work.

☐ teacher

☐ office worker

☐ factory worker

☐ farmer

☐ waiter

☐ shop assistant

☐ nurse

☐ mechanic

☐ policeman

☐ bricklayer

☐ chef

☐ actor

☐ lawyer

jobs

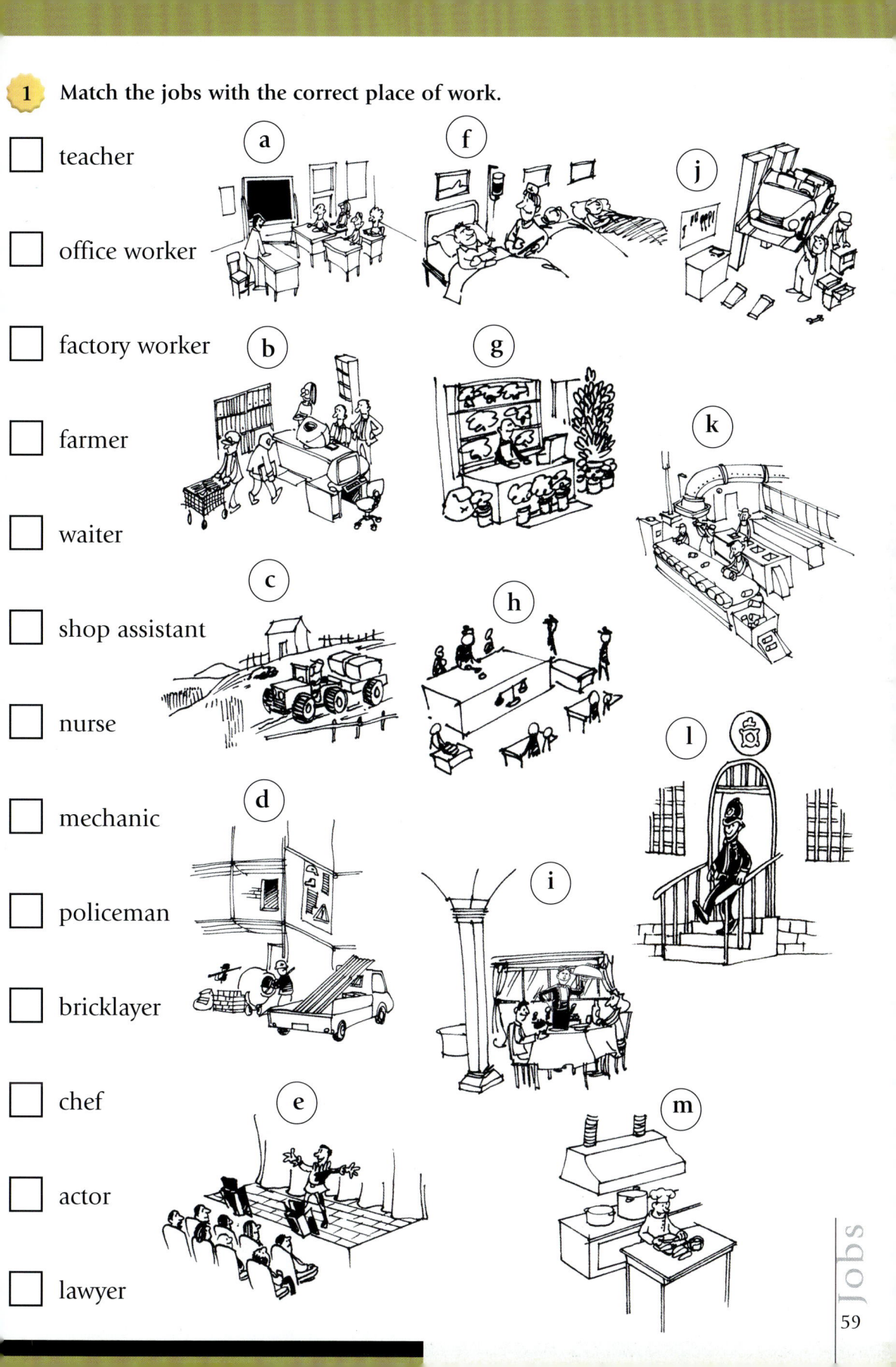

59

2 Find seventeen words in the wordsearch box and then complete the dialogue with the remaining letters.

```
F A C T O R Y W O R K E R I W
A C T O R A R C H I T E C T A
P O L I C E M A N M A T E A I
F E L E C T R I C I A N C H T
A S H O P A S S I S T A N T E
R N E B R I C K L A Y E R R R
M U C A N J O U R N A L I S T
E R H D Y O U I T E A C H E R
R S E M E C H A N I C M A D O
C E F O F F I C E W O R K E R
L A W Y E R T O R D O C T O R
```

Mr Hudson: *What do you do?*
Mr Brown: ....
....
Mr Hudson: ....
Mr Brown: *Pleased to meet you.*

3 What's their job? Complete the sentences.

1. Eric is a ....

2. Nicholas is a ....

3. Victor is an ....

4. Paul is a ....

5. Bob is a ....

6. Mark is a ....

60

4 Do the crossword.

1. This person repairs cars and motorbikes.
2. This person designs houses.
3. This person sits at a desk and uses a computer.
4. This person takes food and drink to people in restaurants.
5. This person looks after patients in hospital.
6. This person works in a shop.
7. This person writes articles for newspapers.
8. This person acts in the theatre.

5 Look at the list of jobs on page 58 and complete the table. Where do they work? Inside or outside?

outside	inside	inside and outside
....	....	....
....	....	....
....	....	....
....	....	....
....	....	....
....	....	....
....	....	....
....	....	....

Now make sentences. For example:

Factory workers work in a factory.

grammar

The Simple Present tense

We use the simple present tense to describe habitual actions. The **affirmative** form of the simple present uses the **infinitive** of the verb, but an 's' is added to the third person singular:

I work.   We work.
You work.   You work.
He/she/it work**s**.   They work.

In the **negative** and **interrogative** forms of the simple present, the auxiliary verb '**do**' is added:

I don't work.   We don't work.
You don't work.   You don't work.
He/she/it doesn't work.   They don't work.

Do I work?   Do we work?
Do you work?   Do you work?
Does he work?   Do they work?

Examples:
Jonathon **goes** to work every day at 9 o'clock.
Susan **doesn't work** in an office.
Where **do they work**?

6 Put in the correct form of the verb.

1. John is a doctor. He .... in a hospital *(work)*.

2. Samantha and Tom are journalists. They .... articles for the Sunday Times. *(write)*

3. Henry repairs cars but he .... motorbikes. *(repair)*

4. I .... food to people in a restaurant. I'm a waiter. *(take)*

5. My sister .... maths, she's a maths teacher. *(like)*

7 Look at the pictures and complete the sentences.

1. Three .... are working on this project.

2. Charlie is a ....

3. I can't go out because I'm waiting for the ....

4. Today there is a meeting with all the ....

5. Luke works as a .... in a restaurant.

6. Dr Smith is my ....

7. The .... are ready to start making the film.

8. There are a lot of .... at the press conference.

9. The .... is going into the court room.

10. Henry would like to be a ....

What job would you like to do?

Jobs

63

The town

traffic lights

street

roundabout

zebra crossing

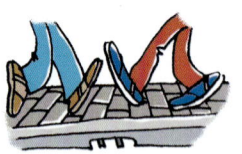

pavement

park

station

bar

shop

supermarket

cinema

bank

post office

school

hotel

hospital

airport

stadium

restaurant

car park

1 Look at the pictures and complete the sentences.

1. This evening we're going to the .... to see a James Bond film.
2. On a Saturday evening I usually go to the .... for a drink with my friends.
3. I'm going to the .... to pick up Mark. His train arrives at 4 o'clock.
4. We're going to Oxford this weekend. We're going to stay in a ....
5. Tomorrow I'm going to the .... to see a football match.
6. We're going to a .... for dinner tonight.

2 What can you see? Write the words in the boxes.

1.
2.
3.
4.
5.

3 Find eight words in the wordsearch box. The remaining letters form a sentence.

```
S U P E R M A R K E T
H O S P I T A L B U S
P C A I R P O R T K H
A I B N G H A M P A O
R L A A S C H O O L P
K C N E I S I N L O N
D O K C A R P A R K N
```

_ _ _ _ _ _ _ _ _ _
_ _ _ _ _ _
_ _ _ _
_ _ _ _ _ _ .

The town

65

4 Do the crossword.

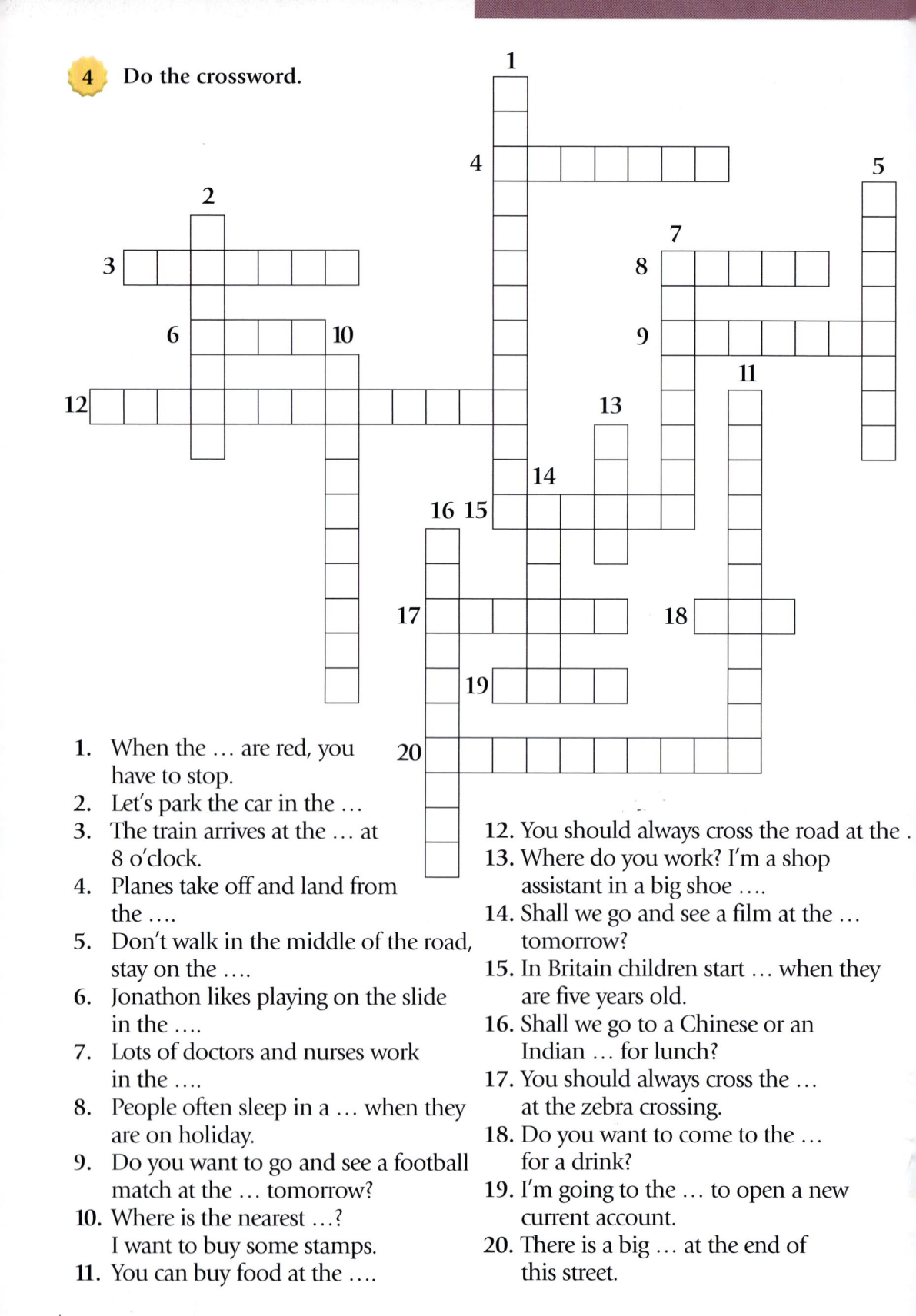

1. When the … are red, you have to stop.
2. Let's park the car in the …
3. The train arrives at the … at 8 o'clock.
4. Planes take off and land from the ….
5. Don't walk in the middle of the road, stay on the ….
6. Jonathon likes playing on the slide in the ….
7. Lots of doctors and nurses work in the ….
8. People often sleep in a … when they are on holiday.
9. Do you want to go and see a football match at the … tomorrow?
10. Where is the nearest …? I want to buy some stamps.
11. You can buy food at the ….
12. You should always cross the road at the .
13. Where do you work? I'm a shop assistant in a big shoe ….
14. Shall we go and see a film at the … tomorrow?
15. In Britain children start … when they are five years old.
16. Shall we go to a Chinese or an Indian … for lunch?
17. You should always cross the … at the zebra crossing.
18. Do you want to come to the … for a drink?
19. I'm going to the … to open a new current account.
20. There is a big … at the end of this street.

66

5 Where are they going? Read the conversations, follow the directions and write the missing word.

1. A: Excuse me, can you tell me the way to the .... ?
   B: Of course, it's easy. Go straight on for about a kilometre. It's on the left after the second set of traffic lights.

2. A: Excuse me, is it far to the .... ?
   B: No, it's not far. Turn right, then turn left and go straight on to the end of the road.

3. A: Excuse me, do you know if there is a .... near here?
   B: Yes, turn left, go straight on to the traffic lights and then turn right. It's on your left.

4. A: Excuse me, do you know where I can find a .... ?
   B: Yes, of course. Turn right and then left and go straight on to the end of the street. It's on your left, opposite the station.

5. A: Excuse me, can you tell me where the .... is?
   B: It's near here. Go straight on for fifty metres then take the first street on the right. It's on the corner.

6. A: Excuse me, do you know where we can find a .... ?
   B: Yes, go straight on and keep going until you reach the first set of traffic lights. Turn right and then go straight on. It's at the end of the road.

The town

67

6 Complete the sentences.

1. Mrs Shepherd is waiting at the ....

2. Paul and Bernard are crossing the road at the ....

3. Mrs Forrester is walking on the ....

7 Where is David's house?

1. David's house is opposite the ....

2. David's house is behind the ....

3. David's house is opposite the ....

4. David's house is beside the ....

5. David's house is to the right of the ....

6. David's house is to the left of the ....

grammar

In or at?

in + street/town/country

She works **in** Burberry Street.
He lives **in** London
They are on holiday **in** France.

at + address

John and Eleanor live **at** 45 Leicester Street.

at + school/the airport/the station/the cinema

John is **at** school.
They are waiting for Jane **at** the station.
Ben's plane is arriving **at** Heathrow airport.
Susie and Fiona are **at** the cinema.

in or at + hotel/restaurant
in and at can both be used with hotel and restaurant.

We are staying **at/in** a hotel tonight.
They are having lunch **at/in** a restaurant.

8 Put in the correct preposition.

1. My sister lives .... Oxford.

2. The train arrives .... the station at 8 o'clock.

3. What hotel are you staying .... ?

4. Birmingham is a city .... England.

5. My brother is .... the cinema this evening.

Transport

plane

car

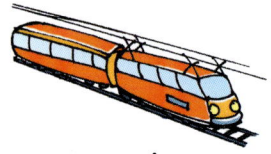

train

bus

tube (train)

bike

motorbike

van

lorry

helicopter

camper

taxi

boat

speedboat

ferry

ship

1 Look at the pictures, complete the sentences and do the crossword.

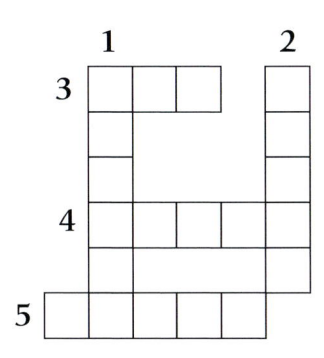

1. Mr and Mrs Robinson usually go on holiday in their ....

2. On Sunday they often go out on their ....

3. Mrs Robinson goes shopping by ....

4. Last year the Robinson family went to the United States by ....

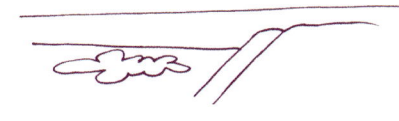

5. Mr Robinson goes to work by ....

Transport

71

2 Find the sixteen words in the wordsearch box then complete the conversation with the remaining letters.

```
S P E E D B O A T N O I D
O N H E L I C O P T E R T
T U B E T R A I N V F C I
U P S C A R S U A A E A L
L L H T R A I N Y N R M G
O A I B U S T O W B R P T
O N P B O A T R K I Y E A
O E L O R R Y N F K O R X
M O T O R B I K E E O T I
```

A: *Do you always go to work by car?*

B: ....
....!

3 Complete the table using the words below.

car   ship   bike   speedboat   lorry
train   tube train   camper   van   taxi
    bus   ferry   boat   motorbike

road	rail	river/sea
....	....	....
....	....	....
....	....	....
....	....	....
....	....	....
....	....	....
....	....	....
....	....	....
....		

Which two means of transport fly in the air?

A _ _ _ _ _ and a _ _ _ _ _ _ _ _ _ _.

4 Look at the pictures and complete the sentences.

1. Michelle is riding her ....

2. Mr Barclay is getting into his ....

3. George and Rose are on the ....

4. Mrs Riley is getting on the ....

5. Mr and Mrs Yates are taking a ....

5 Put in the missing word.

cycling – flying – riding – driving

1. John likes .... his car.

2. Lucy enjoys .... and she has got a new bike.

3. Henry is a pilot and he loves ....

4. Bob hates .... his motorbike in the rain.

Transport

73

grammar

By car or in my car?

*We use **by** to say how we travel.*
To go by + bus/ car/ train/ plane/ ship/ bike

*You can't use **by** when you say **my** car/ **the** train/ **a** taxi. We say:*
in my/his car
on the train
in a taxi

*We use **in** + car/taxi/lorry when we are inside, but **on** + public transport*
on the train
on the bus

*We also say **on** + bike*

6 Put in the correct preposition.

1. Mrs Fisher is going to the dentist .... the tube (train).

2. The Drummond family is going on holiday .... a camper.

3. Mr Smith is going to the coast .... train.

4. Sally usually goes home .... her bike.

5. Angela is going to the station .... her motorbike.

7 Look at the pictures and complete the sentences using the correct form of the verb.

1. The Brown family .... on holiday by car. *(is going/goes)*

2. The plane .... to New York. *(is flying/flies)*

3. Mrs Matthews usually .... home by bus. *(is going/goes)*

4. The children .... their bikes. *(ride/are riding)*

5. Nathan and Vivien always .... a taxi to the theatre. *(take/are taking)*

6. The boys .... the boat. *(are rowing/ row)*

How do you go to school or to your English course?

Transport

The weather and the seasons

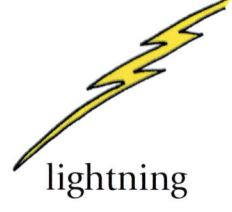

rain

snow

sun

storm

clouds

wind

hailstones

fog

ice

lightning

cold

hot

rainbow

puddle

spring

summer

autumn

winter

1 Do the crossword.

1. December, January and February.
2. June, July and August.
3. September, October and November.
4. March, April and May.

2 Find fourteen words in the wordsearch box. Use the remaining letters to make a question.

....

```
L I G H T N I N G W H R
P S T O R M A T I S T A
U I C E H C L O U D S I
D E W E C O L D F A T N
D H W I N D H E O R S B
L S N O W L O I G K U O
E E T O D A T R A I N W
H A I L S T O N E S Y ?
```

The weather and the seasons

77

3 Look at the pictures and complete the sentences.

1. Put your coat on, it's .... outside.

2. Come and see the .... !

3. Look at those enormous ....

4 What's the weather like? Look at the map and say what the weather is like.

1. London   ....   4. Belfast   ....
2. Edinburgh   ....   5. Cardiff   ....
3. Birmingham   ....   6. Manchester   ....

5 Put the conversations in the correct order.

☐ John: *Hi Mark, where are you?*
☐ John: *It's great, I'm at the pool and it's really hot.*
☐ Mark: *Hello John!*
☐ Mark: *I'm in London and the weather is terrible. What's it like in Miami?*

☐ Jessie: *That's yesterday's newspaper.*
☐ Tom: *But it didn't rain yesterday either!*
☐ Jessie: *It's very hot today!*
☐ Tom: *Yes, but the newspaper says it's going to rain!*

☐ Peter: *Look at those black clouds!*
☐ Jane: *Yes, you're right. It looks like there's going to be a storm.*
☐ Peter: *Let's go home.*
☐ Jane: *Why?*

☐ Ann: *Okay, don't worry!*
☐ Henry: *Hello, where are you?*
☐ Henry: *Drive carefully!*
☐ Ann: *I'm nearly home, but there's a lot of fog!*

The weather and the seasons

79

6 There's a holiday for every season. Look at the pictures and complete the sentences with the four seasons.

1. Susan always goes skiing in the mountains in ....

2. She usually goes for a relaxing weekend by the lake in the ....

3. In the .... she goes to the seaside.

4. The country is her favourite place in ....

7 Look at the pictures and complete the sentences.

1. During a .... there is a lot of ....

2. The .... always leaves big ....

3. When it rains and the .... is in the sky, you can see a ....

grammar

Noun	adjective	
sun	sunny	The **sun** is in the sky, it's a lovely **sunny** day.
fog	foggy	Look at the **fog**! It's so **foggy** outside I can't see.

8 Change the nouns into adjectives.

rain ....
wind ....
snow ....
cloud ....
ice ....

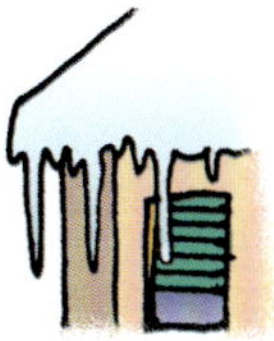

9 What's the weather like? Look at the pictures and choose the correct expression.

It's windy – It's cold – It's raining hailstones – It's sunny
It's hot. – It's foggy – It's snowing – It's a rainy day

1.  It's a rainy day. 5.  ....
2.  .... 6.  ....
3.  .... 7.  ....
4.  .... 8.  ....

The weather and the seasons

81

Actions

eat

drink

listen

work

study

read

write

live

go

get dressed

look

talk

walk

drive

buy

sleep

leave

arrive

open

close

82

1 Complete the sentences.

1. You .... to music with your ears.

2. You .... with your legs.

3. You .... with your mouth.

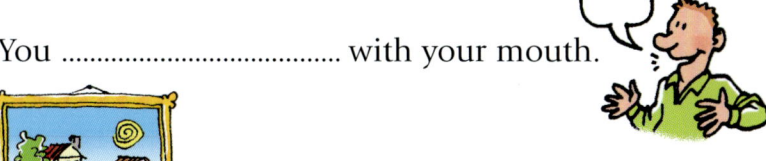

4. You .... at a picture with your eyes.

2 Match the words with the actions.

1. eat   a. at a picture

2. drink   b. a car

3. listen   c. a sandwich

4. read   d. to the cinema

5. write   e. to music

6. look   f. coffee

7. drive   g. a window

8. Go   h. a newspaper

9. open   i. a postcard

Actions

83

3 Do the crossword.

4 Look at the pictures and complete the text with the actions.
Make sure you use the correct form of the verb.

The Adams family .... in Nottingham. Mr Adams has

a shoe shop in the town centre. In the morning he ....

a cup of coffee, gets washed, ... and

.... to work. He .... the shop at 8

o'clock and .... it at half past seven. Mrs Adams doesn't

work. She looks after the house and the children, Stella and Laura.

Stella is the eldest, she is in her first year at university, she is

.... languages and she already .... to her

friends a lot in French and Spanish. Laura is in her first year of primary school.

She is learning to .... and ....

In the evening they all .... dinner together, then

they watch the television and at about 11 o'clock they all

.... to bed.

5 Look at the pictures and complete the sentences using the correct form of the verb.

1. Mr Sinclair .... in a bank. *(work)*

2. Eve .... economics at university. *(study)*

3. Valery usually .... to school. *(walk)*

4. Frank usually .... on the 5 o'clock train. *(leave)*

6 Look at the pictures and complete the sentences.

1. Where .... ?
   In Barker Street.

2. What is Jack doing?
   ....

3. Where is Peter going?
   .... home.

4. How old is Jamie?
   He's ten months old.
   ....?
   Yes, he can.

7 Look at the pictures and make sentences.

get dressed

drive to work

talk to colleagues

1. Phil gets dressed at half past seven.
2. ....
3. ....

talk on the phone

eat lunch

arrive home

4. ....
5. ....
6. ....

eat

read a book

sleep

7. ....
8. ....
9. ....

8 Now describe your typical day.

....
....
....
....
....
....

Actions

Solutions

In the house

Page 5
1 chimney, window, door, garage, roof, wall, garden.
2 bedroom, living room, kitchen, bathroom, study.

Page 6
3 1. bathroom, 2. bedroom, 3. door, 4. roof, 5. garden, 6. living room, 7. study, 8. stairs, 9. wall, 10. hall, 11. window, 12. garage, 13. chimney, 14. cellar, 15. kitchen.

Page 7
4 1. door, 2. garden, 3. cellar, 4. garage, 5. roof, 6. wall, 7. window, 8. chimney, 9. stairs, 10. bedroom.
5 1. bedroom, 2. study, 3. bathroom, 4. kitchen, 5. living room, 6. hall.

Page 8
6 A   There is a living room.
        There is a study.
        There are three bedrooms.

    B   There is a kitchen.
        There is a living room.
        There is a hall.
        There is a study.
        There is a bathroom.
        There are two bedrooms.

Page 9
9 (3) third, (4) fourth, (14) fourteenth, (1) first, (10) tenth. *My house has got a big garden.*

The family

Page 11
1 1. grandfather, 2. cousins, 3. grandchildren, 4. father, 5. son, 6. sister, 7. daughter, 8. uncle, 9. parents, 10. granddaughter, 11. children, 12. husband, 13. grandparents, 14. mother, 15. brother, 16. grandmother, 17. grandson, 18. aunt, 19. wife, 20. nephew, 21. niece.

Page 12
2 1. mother, father; 2. grandfather, grandmother; 3. sister, brother; 4. son, daughter; 5. aunt, uncle; 6. husband, wife; 7. nephew, niece.
3 1. daughter, 2. father, 3. children, 4. husband, 5. brothers, 6. sister.

Page 13
4 aunt, father, mother, uncle, sister, brother, cousin / *There are a lot of relatives and friends at the wedding.*
5 1. mother, 2. father, 3. husband, 4. brother, 5. granddaughter, 6. wife. *My mother's sister is my aunt.*

Page 14
6 1. her, 2. He, 3. They / his, 4. She / their, 5. She / his, 6. He / her, 7. They / his, 8. He / his, 9. He / her, 10. She / her.

Page 15
7 1. his, 2. her, 3. their, 4. their, 5. her, 6. his.

Parts of the body

Page 17
1 leg, head, arm, hand, foot.
2 1. mouth, 2. eyes, 3. ears, 4. nose, 5. hand.

Page 18
3 1. foot, 2. mouth, 3. shoulder, 4. arm, 5. hand, 6. stomach, 7. knee, 8. nose, 9. neck, 10. leg, 11. hair, 12. ear, 13. eye, 14. finger.

Page 19
4 1. head, headache, 2. back, backache, 3. stomach, stomachache, 4. tooth, toothache. *Where does it hurt?*
5 1. hair, 2. nose, 3. hand, 4. ear, 5. finger, 6. arm.

Page 20
6 heads, arms, legs, feet, teeth, fingers mouths / *Parts of the body.*

Page 21
7 arms, legs, ears, eyes, nose, mouth.

Colours

Page 23
1 white, black, red, blue, yellow, green, brown, grey, orange, pink, purple.

Page 24
2 red, blue, yellow, green, white, orange, purple, beige, black, grey, brown, pink. *Have you got a green pen?*
3 1. pink, 2. orange, 3. white, 4. black, 5. red, 6. yellow. *Primary.*

Page 25
4 red, orange, yellow, green, blue, purple, pink.

5 The British flag is red, white and blue.
The Italian flag is green, white and red.
The French flag is blue, white and red.
The German flag is black, red and yellow.
The Spanish flag has two red stripes and one yellow stripe.
The Swiss flag is red with a white cross.

Page 26
6 1. yellow, 2. green, 3. blue, 4. red.
7 1. brown, 2. black, 3. white, 4. green, 5. grey, 6. yellow.

Page 27
8 blue, yellow, green, red, pink, brown, white, purple, black, grey.

Food and drink

Page 29
1 coffee, tea, water, milk, wine.
They are all drinks.
2 1. eggs, 2. pizza, 3. meat, 4. sausages, 5. fruit, 6. vegetables, 7. butter, 8. chicken, 9. rice, 10. cheese, 11. water, 12. fish, 13. ice cream 14. bread.
What do you usually eat at lunch time?

Page 30
3 1. sausages, 2. soup, 3. pizza, 4. rice, 5. butter, 6. fish, 7. milk, 8. chicken, 9. meat, 10. eggs, 11. ice cream, 12. tea, 13. fruit, 14. vegetables, 15. water, 16. coffee, 17. cheese, 18. wine, 19. bread.

Page 31
4 1. cheese, 2. butter, 3. eggs, 4. rice, 5. milk, 6. tea, 7. bread, 8. chicken, 9. vegetables, 10. water.
5 1. cheese, 2. butter, 3. eggs, 4. rice, 5. milk, 6. tea, 7. bread, 8. chicken,

9. vegetables, 10. water. *Mrs Brown is doing the shopping at the supermarket.*

Page 32
6 1. wine 2. fruit 3. pizza, 4. cheese, 5. ice cream, 6. water.
7 1. Right. 2. Wrong: She quite likes fish. 3. Wrong. He doesn't like coffee much. 4. Right. 5. Wrong: They don't like milk at all. 6. Right, 7. Right.

Page 33
8 1. Sheena likes fish. / Sheena doesn't like fish. 2. I like tea a lot. 3. Paul doesn't like cheese at all. 4. They quite like milk. 5. I don't like soup much. 6. We both quite like vegetables. 7. Janet doesn't like coffee at all. 8. They like wine a lot.

Clothes

Page 35
1 1. T-shirt , 2. sweater, 3. trousers, 4. jacket, 5. skirt.
2 1. skirt, 2. pyjamas, 3. shoes, 4. anorak, 5. coat, 6. vest, 7. socks, 8. blouse, 9. raincoat, 10. tie, 11. shirt, 12. jeans, 13. dress/ *I like sports clothes.*

Page 36
3 skirt, trousers, sweater, T-shirt, shoes, socks, shirt, blouse, jacket, dress, jeans, sweatshirt, anorak, coat, raincoat, tie, vest, pants, pyjamas/ *Is there a green one?*
4 A) 1 tie, 2 shirt B) 3 skirt, 4 blouse.

Page 37
5 1. vest, 2. skirt, 3. coat, 4. blouse, 5. pants, 6. dress, 7. T-shirt, 8. sweater/ *Gillian likes wearing trousers.*

6 1. jeans, 2. shoes, 3. socks, 4. tie, 5. shirt/ *Gary likes wearing comfortable shoes.*

Page 38
7 1. tie, 2. raincoat, 3. dress, 4. T-shirt, 5. sweater, 6. trousers, 7. pyjamas, 8. shoes
8 1. tie, 2. raincoat, 3. dress, 4. T-shirt, 5. sweater, 6. trousers, 7. pyjamas, 8. shoes/ *Another way of saying "put on your clothes": Get dressed.*

Page 39
9 I'm taking off my dress. You're taking off your sweater. He's taking off his shirt. We're taking off our socks. You're taking off your shoes. They're taking off their coats.

Animals

Page 41
1 Farm animals: cat, dog, cow, horse, pig, sheep, donkey, hen, rooster.
2 1c, 2g, 3a, 4b, 5d, 6e, 7f.

Page 42
3 1. monkey, 2. rooster, 3. fish, 4. cow, 5. crocodile, 6. giraffe, 7. hen, 8. horse, 9. elephant, 10. lion, 11. dog, 12. donkey, 13. cat, 14. bird, 15. rabbit, 16. sheep, 17. snake, 18. bear, 19. pig.

Page 43
4 horse, hen, pig, rabbit, sheep, fish, cow / *cat.*
5 1. giraffe, 2. cat, 3. dog, 4. cow, 5. rabbit, 6. rooster, 7. hen, 8. sheep, 9. bird, 10. fish, 11. snake, 12. pig.

Page 44
6 She swims like a fish! He eats like a horse! He is the black sheep of the family! It's a dog's life! She's crying crocodile tears!

7 cow, horse, cow, hen, hen, pig, fish, horse, pig, fish.

Page 45
8 1. A donkey is more stubborn than a rabbit.
2. A giraffe is taller than a monkey.
3. A monkey is more intelligent than a hen.
4. A sheep is smaller than a cow.
5 A bear is more dangerous than a rooster.
6. A horse can run faster than a donkey.
7. A lion is more ferocious than a cat.
8. A crocodile is slower than a rabbit.

Nature

Page 47
1 1. flower, 2. lake, 3. field, 4. sky, 5. sun, 6. tree.
2 mountains, island, sky, moon, lake, river, sun, sea, field, country, hills, woods, flower, star, tree/*No more pollution!*

Page 48
3 tree, woods, lake, mountains, sun, sky, flower, field, sea, hills, river, country.
4 *I can see the moon and the stars.*

Page 49
5 1. Lake, 2. island, 3. river, 4. mountain.
6 1. flower 2. tree, 3. mountains, 4. woods, 5. country, 6. hills.
7 sun, sky, fields, flowers, moon, stars.

Page 50
8 I can see the sea, the sun, the sky, an island. I can see the mountains, a lake, the woods, the sky.
9 country, mountains, sun, woods, flowers, lake, moon, stars, sky.

Page 51
10 1. Can/moon, 2. want/country, 3. can/sea, 4. Can/lake, 5. want/mountains.

At school

Page 53
1 1. blackboard, 2. bin, 3. backpack, 4. desk, 5. chair
2 1. pencil, 2. desk, 3. bin, 4. classroom, 5. sticky tape, 6. ruler, 7. blackboard, 8. paper, 9. scissors, 10. eraser/ *What colour is your pencil case?*

Page 54
3 1. pen, 2. diary, 3. ruler, 4. pencil case, 5. exercise book, 6. book, 7. paper, 8. eraser.
4 blackboard, backpack, bin, desk, diary, paper, eraser, sticky tape, pencil, scissors, ruler, book, exercise book, classroom, felt pen, pen, glue stick, pencil case/ *Do you enjoy going to school?*

Page 55
5 1. blackboard, 2. felt pens, 3. book, 4. classroom.
6 1. pen, 2. eraser, 3. pencil sharpener, 4. ruler, 5. scissors.
7 1c, 2a, 3d, 4b

Page 56
8 1. blackboard, 2. pencil, 3. glue stick, 4. scissors, 5. classroom, 6. eraser, 7. desk, 8. pencil case, 9. paper, 10. ruler.

Page 57
9 1. Don't talk, 2. Open, 3. Put, 4. Don't sit, 5. Let's go, 6. Listen, 7. Write, 8. Let's have.

Jobs

Page 59
1 (a) teacher, (b) office worker, (k) factory worker, (c) farmer, (i) waiter, (g) shop assistant, (f) nurse, (j) mechanic, (l) policeman, (d) bricklayer, (m) chef, (e) actor, (h) lawyer.

Page 60
2 factory worker, actor, architect, waiter, farmer, policeman, electrician, shop assistant, bricklayer, journalist, teacher, chef, nurse, mechanic, office worker, lawyer, doctor / *I'm a teacher and you? I'm a doctor.*
3 1. chef, 2. policeman, 3. electrician, 4. teacher, 5. doctor, 6. lawyer.

Page 61
4 1. mechanic, 2. architect, 3. office worker, 4. waiter, 5. nurse, 6. shop assistant, 7. journalist, 8. actor.
5 *Outside:* farmer, bricklayer.
Inside: teacher, office worker, factory worker, waiter, shop assistant, doctor, mechanic, nurse, chef, lawyer, actor.
Inside and outside: architect, policeman, electrician, journalist.

Page 62
6 1. works 2. write 3. doesn't repair 4. take 5. likes.

Page 63
7 1. architects, 2. shop assistant, 3. electrician, 4. teachers, 5. waiter, 6. doctor, 7. actors, 8. journalists, 9. lawyer, 10. policeman.

The town

Page 65
1 1. cinema, 2. bar, 3. station, 4. hotel, 5. stadium, 6. restaurant.
2 1. roundabout, 2. park, 3. pavement, 4. street, 5. zebra crossing.
3 supermarket, hospital, airport, school, car park, park, shop, bank /
Buckingham Palace is in London.

Page 66
4 1. traffic lights, 2. car park, 3. station, 4. airport, 5. pavement, 6. park, 7. hospital, 8. hotel, 9. stadium, 10. post office, 11. supermarket, 12. zebra crossing, 13. shop, 14. cinema, 15. school, 16. restaurant, 17. street, 18. bar, 19. bank, 20. roundabout.

Page 67
5 1. hospital, 2. station, 3. supermarket, 4. post office, 5. cinema, 6. hotel.

Page 68
6 1. traffic lights, 2. zebra crossing, 3. pavement.
7 1. cinema, 2. car park, 3. post office, 4. bar, 5. supermarket, 6. bank.

Page 69
8 1. in, 2. at, 3. in/at, 4. in, 5. at.

Transport

Page 71
1 1. camper, 2. bikes, 3. car, 4. plane, 5. train.

Page 72
2 speedboat, helicopter, tube train, car, bus, train, boat, lorry, motorbike, plane,

Solutions

93

ship, bike, ferry, camper, taxi, van.
A: Do you always go to work by car?
B: No, I don't, I usually go to work on foot!
3 *Road:* car, bus, bike, lorry, motorbike, camper, taxi, van.
Rail: train, tube train.
River/sea: ship, ferry, boat, speedboat.
A plane and a helicopter.

Page 73
4 1. bike, 2. car, 3. train, 4. bus, 5. taxi.
5 1. driving, 2. cycling, 3. flying, 4. riding.

Page 74
6 1. on, 2. in, 3. by, 4. on, 5. on.

Page 75
7 1. is going, 2. is flying, 3. goes,
4. are riding, 5. take 6. are rowing

The weather and the seasons

Page 77
1 1. winter, 2. summer, 3. autumn, 4. spring.
2 lightning, storm, ice, clouds, cold, wind, snow, rain, hailstones, puddle, hot, fog, sun, rainbow. *What is the weather like today?*

Page 78
3 1. cold, 2. snow, 3. hailstones.
4 1. sun, 2. snow, 3. wind, 4. rain, 5. storm, 6. clouds.

Page 79
5   Mark: *Hello John!*
    John: *Hi Mark, where are you?*
    Mark: *I'm in London and the weather is terrible. What's it like in Miami?*
    John: *It's great, I'm at the pool and it's really hot.*

Jessie: *It's very hot today!*
Tom: *Yes, but the newspaper says it's going to rain!*
Jessie: *That's yesterday's newspaper.*
Tom: *But it didn't rain yesterday either!*

Peter: *Let's go home*
Jane: *Why?*
Peter: *Look at those black clouds!*
Jane: *Yes, you're right. It looks like there's going to be a storm.*

Henry: *Hello, where are you?*
Ann: *I'm nearly home, but there's a lot of fog!*
Henry: *Drive carefully!*
Ann: *Okay, don't worry!*

Page 80
6 1. winter, 2. spring, 3. summer, 4. autumn.
7 1. storm, lightning, 2. rain, puddles, 3. sun, rainbow

Page 81
8 rainy, windy, snowy, cloudy, icy.
9 1. It's a rainy day. 2. It's cold. 3. It's snowing. 4. It's sunny. 5. It's windy. 6. It's raining hailstones. 7. It's foggy. 8. It's hot.

Actions

Page 83
1 1. listen, 2. walk, 3. talk, 4. look.
2 1c, 2f, 3e, 4h, 5i, 6a, 7b, 8d, 9g.

Page 84
3 1. buy, 2. sleep, 3. study, 4. go, 5. talk, 6. drink, 7. get dressed, 8. write, 9. look, 10. walk, 11. work, 12. live, 13. listen, 14. arrive, 15. eat, 16. read, 17. close, 18. drive, 19. leave, 20. open.

Page 85
4 lives, drinks, gets dressed, goes, opens, closes, studying, talks, read, write, eat, go.

Page 86
5 1. works, 2. studies, 3. walks 4. leaves.
6 1. Where do you live? 2. He's sleeping.
3. He's going home.
4. Can he walk?

Page 87
7 1. Phil gets dressed at half past seven.
2. He drives to work at eight o'clock.
3. He talks to his colleagues at half past eight.
4. He talks on the phone at ten o'clock.
5. He eats lunch at one o'clock.
6. He arrives home at six o'clock.
7. He eats dinner at eight o'clock.
8. He reads a book at ten o'clock.
9. He sleeps at eleven o'clock.

Contents

In the house	page 4
The family	10
Parts of the body	16
Colours	22
Food and drink	28
Clothes	34
Animals	40
Nature	46
At school	52
Jobs	58
The town	64
Transport	70
The weather and the seasons	76
Actions	82
Solutions	89